STAR HOTEL

& SILK

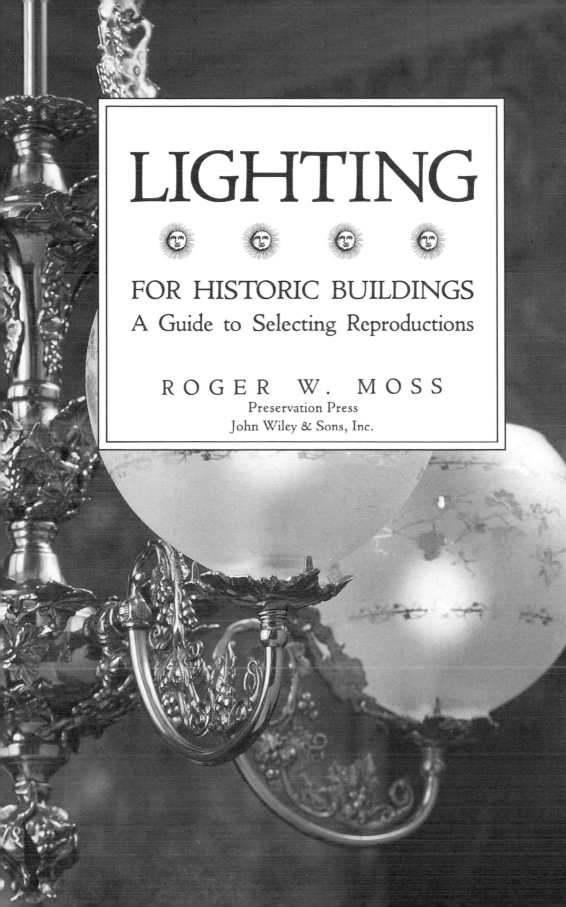

LIGHTING

FOR HISTORIC BUILDINGS
A Guide to Selecting Reproductions

ROGER W. MOSS

Preservation Press
John Wiley & Sons, Inc.

Printed in the United States of America
9

Library of Congress Cataloging in Publication Data

Moss, Roger W., 1940–
     Lighting for historic buildings : a guide to selecting
  reproductions / Roger W. Moss.
          p.   cm.
     Bibliography: p.
     ISBN 0-471-14399-5
     1. Lighting, Architectural and decorative—Catalogs.
     2. Historic buildings—Lighting—Catalogs.   I. Title.
NK2115.5.L5M67   1988
749'.63'02973—dc 19   87-36012

Preservation Press gratefully acknowledges the assistance of Progress Lighting in the production of the cover.

Cover and title page: ROCOCO GAS CHANDELIER, 1850s. Progress Lighting. (See page 117.)

Endleaves: Street lighting, c. 1904, as depicted in a Walter Macfarlane Company catalog, Glasgow, Scotland. (The Dornsife Collection of the Victorian Society in America at The Athenaeum of Philadelphia)

Pages 8–9: *The Harden Family at Brathay Hall*, 1827, by John Harden (detail). Family members rely on natural light for indoor activities. (Abbot Hall Art Gallery, Kendal, Westmorland)

Pages 28–29: *Interior of Peale's Museum*, 1822, by Titian Peale. Argand-burner hanging fixtures illuminate the gallery. (Founders Society, Detroit Institute of Arts)

CONTENTS

INTRODUCTION

CATALOG OF
REPRODUCTION
LIGHTING

LIGHTING FOR HISTORIC BUILDINGS

A Guide to Selecting Reproductions

INTRODUCTION

LIGHTING FOR
HISTORIC BUILDINGS

Lighting a historic building—from a home to a public building or museum—poses a multitude of vexing problems not encountered when re-creating the more decorative aspects of period interiors. The color, texture and pattern of historic paints, wallpapers, carpets and window treatments can be reasonably simulated, but duplicating historic light levels and fixtures is more complex.

LEVELS OF LIGHT

Natural light is the most authentic illumination for historic buildings constructed before the mid-19th century. The pattern of daily life and work, the arrangement of furniture, the colors, fabrics and finishing techniques used for interior decoration were all determined in part by the half of every day that most people lived in darkness—darkness only barely relieved by the meager light of fireplace, candle or oil lamp. One of the most dramatic and fundamental changes in Western architecture and interior design occurred when artificial light became the primary source of illumination. Because few 20th-century homeowners and curators would or could accept the daily limitations of life dependent on sunlight, most historic interiors will not be authentically illuminated. Even if the homeowner or curator wanted to cope with rooms illuminated by candles, oil, burning fluid, gas or kerosene, a host of necessary regulations designed to protect building occupants stand in the way.

SAFETY CONCERNS. Modern building codes, especially for public structures, do not permit the use of pre-electrical energy sources as the primary illumination. In addition to the overriding concern for protecting human

Original 1847 gaseliers and wall brackets in the Main Reading Room of The Athenaeum of Philadelphia (1845), now wired for electricity. These fixtures are also tied to a natural gas emergency generator and fitted with rheostats to regulate light levels. (The Athenaeum of Philadelphia)

11

life and property from fire, the use of open flame is not practical for more than decorative lighting, even in a private residence. Nor is protection from fire the only consideration. Modern standards for lighting public spaces require both emergency lighting (via a generator operated from an alternative energy source or battery pack) and light levels—usually expressed in footcandles— that normally exceed those achievable by pre-electrical energy sources. Also, unless the building is to have sup- plemental lighting, original or reproduction fixtures that are technologically and stylistically appropriate must be wired for electricity.

Of course, there are ways around some of these prob- lems. At The Athenaeum of Philadelphia (1845, John Notman), a National Historic Landmark near Indepen- dence Hall, the original gaseliers have been wired for electricity. By placing each room on a master rheostat, the light levels can be raised or lowered according to need: low levels for receptions and chamber-music con- certs, when it is desirable to simulate the original gas- light, and high levels when the spaces are being cleaned. Additionally, the fixtures have been tied to a natural gas emergency generator that automatically takes over if the electrical power fails. This type of system eliminates the need in a historic building for obtrusive, battery-powered emergency lights that must satisfy local electrical codes for public structures. Even with such a sophisticated and expensive system, however, illuminated exit signs that glow conspicuously are required for buildings open to the public. However much the preservationist may decry intrusions such as exit lighting and brightly illuminated stairs, they are modern facts of life that cannot be ignored.

HISTORIC LIGHT LEVELS. Unfortunately, the requirement of adequate lighting is too often an argu- ment for installing excessive levels of ambient (overall) illumination, usually in the form of recessed ceiling fix- tures. Many historic buildings rehabilitated in the past two decades—particularly institutional structures—are now outfitted with enough downlights, wall washers and intrusive track lighting to supply a dealer's showroom. It is not uncommon to find the ceilings of these buildings defaced with more holes than a slice of Swiss cheese, each opening concealing a 150-watt bulb that assails the visitor with unnecessary and unhistorical light.

Whatever supplemental lighting that is required for safety in public buildings should be sensitively introduced in a manner that will neither deface the architecture nor alter the way in which the original builder or architect expected the space to be seen. To reproduce faithfully fabrics and wall colors selected originally to be viewed by natural light or by the low levels of nighttime illumination provided by candles, mantel lamps, wall sconces or hanging fixtures and then to flood these surfaces with modern light levels adequate for an operating theater grossly distorts the interpretation of these colors and finishes. Even the historical arrangement of furniture and the importance of reflective surfaces—gilded picture frames, mirrors and highly polished wood, for example— become unintelligible under unblinking incandescent or fluorescent light. Modern light sources also change the way the human eye perceives color. Incandescent light enhances the red end of the color spectrum, and most fluorescent lights enhance the blue end of the spectrum.

Matters of safety aside, homeowners and curators will doubtless object to adopting historic light levels. However, the curator must balance historical authenticity and the understandable desire to have visitors see and appreciate all the objects in a room, not just those that happen to be within reach of carefully filtered natural light.

DAMAGING EFFECTS OF LIGHT. The potential damage from light should likewise be considered, particularly its effects on textiles, paper, wood, paintings, leather and other organic materials. The rate of light damage is proportional to the amount of exposure; cutting the time of exposure in half, for example, reduces the damage by half. Daylight coming through unfiltered windows normally measures 125 footcandles; however, recommended light levels for textiles (costumes, tapestries, window hangings, upholstery and carpets), paper (watercolors, prints, drawings and wallpaper) and similar materials is only 5 footcandles. And light levels on oil and tempera paintings should not exceed 15 footcandles.

All light is damaging, but ultraviolet radiation can

cause structural damage as well as fading. Because the short wavelengths of ultraviolet radiation are invisible, they can be eliminated by filters without reducing the perception of light in the room. These filters may take the form of special sheet Plexiglass installed in place of or over window glass, polyester plastic sheets that can be attached to the inside of windows, polyester screens installed on rollers to be pulled down when needed or—most satisfactory of all—a liquid film applied to the glass. Incandescent light is relatively low in ultraviolet radiation, but fluorescent lamps are second only to daylight as a source of harmful light. Consequently, fluorescent lamps installed in areas where vulnerable materials are displayed or stored should always be screened by relatively inexpensive filters that slip over the tubes.

Low-voltage electrification of period fixtures and lamps is a popular solution for lighting museum sites, yet it may encourage the introduction of more light sources than would be historically appropriate. Wiring museum-quality period fixtures and lamps may also destroy burners that have survived in original condition. Rather than wire unaltered antiques, suitable reproductions should be used, or antiques that have lost their original burners may be wired for electricity. Other solutions include equipping docents with flashlights to direct visitors' attention to important objects in a room or installing unobtrusive supplemental lighting that the self-guided visitor can activate along with a recorded explanation after entering the room and experiencing the historic light levels. These supplemental lights might be portable spots at floor level or permanent fixtures located above and behind the viewer. All of these techniques are more or less acceptable compromises in a museum setting.

Although contemporary Americans have come to expect residential interiors that are lighted, warmed and cooled to the point where it is nearly impossible to determine the season or time of day, those living in historic houses need to give as much thought to lighting their homes as they do to other aspects of interior decoration. For instance, the level of ambient illumination from intrusive modern fixtures can be reduced in favor of more energy-efficient and appropriate task lighting from

opposite top
Determining the appropriate level of light with a handheld light meter. Shielded 40-watt, low-temperature incandescent fluorescent tubes illuminate the case, while a special acrylic sheet, designed to filter out ultraviolet radiation of 400 nanometers and below, protects the drawing. (Louis Meehan, The Athenaeum of Philadelphia)

opposite bottom
Installing ultraviolet light shields on fluorescent tubes. Ultraviolet rays can split the long, interlocking chains of cellulose molecules in paper, causing brittleness and discoloration. (Louis Meehan, The Athenaeum of Philadelphia)

original or reproduction lamps and fixtures that have been wired for electricity.

SELECTING APPROPRIATE LIGHTING FIXTURES

Determining the level of light and the type and number of light sources that are appropriate for a given historic interior begins with an appreciation of lighting technology. For example, colonial-era household inventories, commonly taken at the time of an occupant's death to settle the estate, provide an often startling insight into how little artificial lighting was typically available before the widespread adoption of gas, kerosene and electricity. Kerosene-fueled lighting did not become common in America until after the opening of the Pennsylvania oil fields on the eve of the Civil War. Hollywood set designers notwithstanding, prewar Tara could not have been illuminated by those kerosene *Gone with the Wind* lamps so beloved by glass collectors. Nor would a house built beyond local gas mains be a likely candidate for gas lighting unless the owners had been prosperous enough to have their own generating plant. Economic standing in the community was, of course, a factor regardless of the period, but modern-day owners of 17th- and 18th-century houses may be distressed to learn that chandeliers rarely appear in residential inventories from the colonial period. Most of the reproductions and adaptations listed in the catalog here are reproduced from surviving examples used in such public structures as meeting houses. Not a few owners of low-ceilinged colonial houses have been frustrated by attempts to introduce a chandelier appropriate in scale for a Congregational church into a room now used for dining. Estate inventories suggest that table-top task lighting and sidewall sconces were far more typical.

Throughout this book lighting fixtures are categorized by the fuel or energy source on which they originally depended rather than by style. The style of pre-electric lamps and lighting fixtures is incidental to the primary purpose of the object: to deliver the fuel to a more or less controlled flame. For this reason a Coca-Cola bottle fitted with a wick and burner is just as effective a kerosene lamp as the most handsome and collectible ruby-cut-

to-clear product of the Boston and Sandwich Glass Company. Once this perspective is adopted some of the most common errors of selecting and installing lighting in historic buildings can be avoided.

COMMON ERRORS OF INSTALLATION. In too many house museums and private homes electrified gas fixtures are suspended from chains. More than one curator has blushed bright red when asked, "How do you suppose the gas got to that fixture?" To achieve an authentic look, gas fixtures must be suspended from pipes, and most of the manufacturers listed in the pages that follow will provide additional tubing of the same finish as their fixtures for a modest charge. Most fixtures are supplied with a minimum length and a maximum, or normal, length. If the ceiling height permits, the fixture should be ordered in the longer length together with the necessary

The Long Gallery of Independence Hall (1732–55), with early 18th-century chandeliers reproduced by Ball and Ball. One of the middle chandeliers is the document. (National Park Service)

extra tubing, which can be joined to the fixture by a simple, double-threaded coupling.

But how high should such fixtures be hung? The typical chandelier, gaselier or hall light should be suspended no more than 78 to 84 inches from the floor to the bottom of the fixture—just clearance enough to allow a tall person to walk beneath it comfortably. Because a 12-foot ceiling is 144 inches high—not an unusual height for houses of the 19th century—and most fixtures average about 30 inches long, a chain or pipe of approximately 36 inches will be needed to fill the gap. A 30-inch fixture mounted directly on the ceiling would be more than 9 feet off the floor. (Pity the person who had to light those candles or turn on those gas cocks and light the burners, even with a 3-foot-long torch-and-key lighter!) Naturally, these measurements will require adjustment depending on the ceiling height and the overall length of the fixture. Another consideration is that hanging ceiling fixtures too high distorts the relationship between the light source and furnishings, encourages unhistorical light intensity and places what may be a major decorative feature so high in the room that it cannot be appreciated.

Another common error is hanging inappropriate fixtures in passages and vestibules where a puff of wind from an open exterior door would have immediately extinguished an exposed flame. Household estate inventories often list a glass-enclosed lantern hanging in these locations. Protection from drafts was especially needed in houses originally lighted by candles and oil lamps. Hanging electrified "candle" fixtures in such locations advertises a failure to appreciate the limitations of open-flame technology.

Gaslight levels were usually greater than those provided by candles or oil lamps, but far lower than what Americans of the late 20th century are used to. Generally, an illuminated fishtail or batswing gas burner equalled approximately 16 candlepower. Consequently, the lamps (bulbs) used in electrified gas fixtures should not be more than 10 watts for each burner being simulated. Most electrically wired reproductions and adaptations listed in this book come fitted with sockets for 60- to 100-watt bulbs, and homeowners typically use bulbs of this size. Yet a four-light gaselier with four 60-watt bulbs totals 240 watts instead of the 40 watts that historically would have been possible from a similar fixture burning gas. The simplest solution, as suggested earlier, is a rheostat, which can easily be installed in place of the modern wall switch. If higher levels of light are needed—when cleaning, for instance—the dimmer can be turned up.

A similar problem is faced when installing early electric fixtures designed to use clear glass bulbs with carbon "hairpin" filaments. The light from one of these bulbs (c. 1880s to c. 1910) was considerably lower than the modern 60-watt bulb. Consequently, owners or curators will probably want to acquire reproduction carbon-filament bulbs for use in early electric fixtures, especially if the bulbs are exposed to view. The modern bulb with a tungsten filament and frosted interior did not become generally available until the 1920s.

RESEARCH. Determining the type and style of lighting fixtures appropriate for a historic building depends on minute sifting of primary sources. The date of original construction and any subsequent additions or renovations as well as information on how the structure was decorated should be compiled from a chain of title, insurance atlases and plat maps, tax records, wills and inventories, family papers and early photographs, which may be in the possession of local historical societies or descendants of former owners.

Selection of the interpretive date will largely determine the lighting technologies that are appropriate. A target date of about 1800 will probably limit the fixtures to those designed to burn candles or whale oil, while a date of about 1850 may extend the choice to allow for fixtures fueled by burning fluid, lard oil or gas. A post–Civil War date permits the use of kerosene fixtures, and late 1880s structures might have electric or gas-electric combination fixtures as well. All of these choices will depend on the economic level of the household being studied, its geographical location and the date that public gas or electrical generating systems became available.

The structure also needs to be carefully examined for physical evidence that may indicate how the interior was illuminated. Capped gas pipes, remnants of surface-mounted electrical installations or surviving fixtures in less public areas such as upper floors and cellars should be sought, while the presence of wrought-iron hooks in the center of parlor ceilings may suggest earlier lighting technology. Because a building erected 200 years ago will probably have had its lighting upgraded several times, the target date selected will be important and may even be changed on the basis of what survives. Is the structure to be taken back to its earliest technology or to a later one? If original gas fixtures installed about 1850 survive in an 1810 structure, it might be desirable to select the later date for the furnishing or interpretation plan rather than remove the fixtures in favor of reproductions of the earlier style.

Once all this information is gathered, the homeowner, decorator, architect or curator can turn to other primary sources to learn more about appropriate fixtures. Prints, paintings, watercolors and photographs of similar structures of the period will suggest that the typical interior usually enjoyed a mixture of technologies: a middle-class household of 1845 might well have illuminated the parlor with a single solar lamp burning lard oil and elsewhere have used candles. A similar parlor from 1870 might have been illuminated by a gaselier and wall brackets with portable kerosene lamps for task lighting, and it is not uncommon to find interiors from 1900 furnished with gas-electric combination hanging fixtures and kerosene banquet lamps.

ORIGINAL FIXTURES. If the owner is fortunate, the original lighting fixtures will have survived. The gaseliers and wall brackets at The Athenaeum of Philadelphia, for example, were illuminated by gas from 1847 until 1923, when they were wired for electricity and updated by simply cutting off the gas cocks, removing the shade rings and shades, and fitting each arm with a cardboard "candle" to hide the electrical socket. Restoration required removing the cardboard candles and installing appropriate fittings and shades. Had the gas fixtures been replaced in 1923 with the latest electrical design, The Athenaeum would have been forced to decide among four courses: to retain the later installation, to locate antique gas fixtures of the 1840s, to commission custom reproductions based on photographic evidence or to acquire whatever early gas-style reproductions were readily available from lighting manufacturers.

Unfortunately, as lighting technology changed in the 19th century, it was easier to replace outdated fixtures than to convert them. Consequently, it is rare to find pre-electric lighting in situ. Early fixtures that might have been stored in attics, basements and barns became prime targets for scrap-metal drives during World War I and World War II, and thousands of chandeliers, gaseliers, wall brackets and hall lanterns were broken up and melted down for home-front contributions to the war effort. Those period fixtures that do survive are relatively scarce and accordingly expensive in the antiques market, especially in sets, and it is even less common to find the original glass shades. The catalog here lists a number of dealers who specialize in antique lighting fixtures, but in most cases—especially where sets of pre-electric fixtures are sought—it is necessary to purchase ready-made reproductions or to commission custom reproductions, which can be painfully expensive.

USING REPRODUCTIONS

Changes in scale to fit modern tastes and manufacturing techniques are rampant throughout the reproduction industry, including items such as wallpapers and floor coverings. As with reproductions of other furnishings, lighting manufacturers are not above making such changes or copying a popular item in a competitor's line, perhaps modifying the scale and adapting the design to use an element (candle cup, arm, back plate) for which they already have a pattern. There is nothing illegal in this practice, but each time a fixture is copied it may drift further from the original model, or document. Even when a fixture is known to be based on a document that has survived in situ since the 18th or 19th century, it may be offered by several manufacturers in a range of scales and finishes, all labeled "reproduction." An example is the famous Carpenters' Hall sconce. The original of this handsome, mirror-back fixture is 24 inches high, appropriate in scale to the rooms where the First Continental

Sconce, c. 1840, pro-
duced by A. J. Nash,
Cornhill, London. This
sconce is the document
for the reproduction
illustrated on page 23.

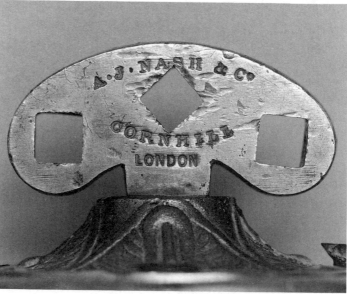

A. J. Nash's maker's
mark on the c. 1840
sconce.

Price Glover's "Nash Triple Arm" (No. PGR-110; see page 71), almost an exact reproduction of the c. 1840 sconce.

Congress met in Philadelphia during those fateful early days of the Revolution. Yet many of the fixtures adapted from the Carpenters' Hall sconce are substantially smaller than the document because the manufacturers believe that modern homeowners would not purchase such large-scale fixtures.

In recent years a number of historic sites and museums—Colonial Williamsburg being the best known—have entered into licensing agreements with manufacturers of lighting fixtures. The museum is paid a percentage of the sales price, and the consumer has curatorial assurance that the product is an accurate, line-for-line reproduction of a document in the museum's collection or is an authorized adaptation. The unauthorized use of an institutional name is prohibited by law, and a manufacturer using one does so at the peril of receiving a stern letter from the museum's lawyer.

Art Nouveau gaselier from the Gibson Gas Fixture Works catalog, Philadelphia, c. 1908. Note the small size of the fitting, which joins the vertical gas pipe and the arms. (The Athenaeum of Philadelphia)

opposite
Modern four-arm reproduction of the Gibson Gas fixture by Progress Lighting (No. P-4041; see page 109) installed at the Queen Victoria Inn, Cape May, N.J. The larger fitting accommodates an approved electrical connection.

However, the fixtures mentioned in this book that do not bear an institutional imprimatur may be as acceptable for use in historic buildings as those licensed by a historic site or museum. In several instances the products are carefully scaled from photographs of museum documents and reproduced without permission of the owner. When that source or a similar source is known to the author, it is cited in the catalog as a guide to the reader who may wish to see a similar original. The inclusion of this information does not mean that the manufacturer is claiming title to a licensing agreement or that the manufacturer is using the name of the owner, to which it is legally not entitled. When a licensing agreement does exist, the catalog entry makes this clear.

GAPS IN AVAILABLE REPRODUCTIONS. Our knowledge of lighting technology has not kept pace with the study of other decorative aspects of interior-design history. The majority of books on lighting aim mainly at collectors of brass, silver and glass objects rather than at those persons interested in the relationship between lighting technology and historic buildings. As the historic preservation movement has grown, manufacturers of fabrics, wallpapers, paints, carpets, plaster moldings, floor tiles, furniture and a host of other products have rushed in to supply a burgeoning market—a market in which the manufacturer with the most authentic reproduction has proved to have an edge on the competition.

Accurate reproductions of 18th- and early 19th-century candle fixtures and late 19th-century gas or gas-electric fixtures are easier to obtain than those that came between. No American manufacturer currently offers reproduction whale-oil, burning-fluid or lard-oil solar fixtures of the type that would be appropriate for the first half of the 19th century, and only a few pre–Civil War gas fixtures and early kerosene fixtures of the 1860s and 1870s are available. In part this is because these fixtures require cast and turned elements that are expensive to reproduce, finish and assemble. Also, they demand glass chimneys and shades that require special molds and cutting techniques that are generally beyond the capabilities of domestic manufacturers.

As the demand for accurate reproductions grows, it is

hoped that the gaps in lighting reproductions indicated in the following chapters will be filled.

NECESSARY ADAPTATIONS. Reproduction lighting fixtures—especially gas and gas-electric fixtures—are rarely exact, line-for-line copies of originals. This is so primarily because of the need to meet the requirements of the Underwriters Laboratories. For example, a simple "T" (T-shaped) gas fixture is nothing more than a vertical gas pipe terminating in a fitting that allows two arms to go off at right angles. Because the electrical wire of a modern reproduction must make a right-angle turn at that joint, the modern coupling may be slightly larger than the original to allow for an approved connection. Also, because of the need to provide an electrical socket in place of the candle or burner, the relationship of arm, shade fitter and shade may also be altered slightly, just as the size of back plates supplied with many wall brackets has been enlarged by the manufacturer to cover the modern electrical box. The better manufacturers are aware of these problems, just as some are aware that a gas cock is needed for an authentic gas or gas-electric fixture. The prospective purchaser should compare unaltered fixtures with reproductions before making a purchase. The information sources and bibliography at the back of the book list major collections of lighting fixtures that may be visited and the many books available on various aspects of lighting history.

FINISHES. The manufacturers of candle fixtures have gone to great lengths to simulate successfully the oxidized finishes of early tinned sheet-iron, wrought-iron and brass surfaces. The more complex finishes used by large-scale 19th-century manufacturers such as Cornelius and Company (later Cornelius and Baker) and Archer and Warner, however, are rarely matched, especially those that combine matte gilt, antique bronze and brightly highlighted elements. The purchaser who seeks reproductions of these combination finishes will be frustrated.

GLASS SHADES. It is also difficult to acquire appropriate glass shades for both surviving period fixtures and reproductions. The diameter of pre-Centennial gas-fixture shades was usually 2½ inches at the neck (where the shade was held to the arm by a ring or "fitter"), but most manufacturers of reproductions supply their fixtures with wider, 3 1/2- or 4 1/4-inch-neck shades that are suitable for later periods. The first manufacturer who develops a line of high-quality, small-neck shades in appropriate patterns will find a brisk demand for the product from both modern manufacturers and owners of period lighting fixtures.

HOW TO USE THE CATALOG

The following catalog of reproduction and adaptation lighting fixtures is arranged in five chapters based on the original energy source (candle; whale oil, lard oil and burning fluid; kerosene; gas; and electricity). Each of these chapters is further divided by fixture type, e.g., chandelier, lantern, sconce. (No effort has been made to list the hundreds of reproduction candlesticks and candelabra that are not normally electrified or the table-top oil and kerosene lamps that are readily available in the antiques market.) A sixth chapter lists specialty items and services, such as firms that locate antiques, create custom fixtures and provide products such as candles, crystal prisms and reproduction light bulbs, switches and shades. A final chapter covers street lighting.

Individual catalog entries give the following information when it is available:

Manufacturer's name

Catalog or descriptive name for the fixture

Brief description including style, number of arms and lights, materials and finishes

Geographical origin and date of the design

Dimensions

Information about the source of the design, including original documents

Bibliographic references to illustrations

Product number or numbers

Special ordering information

Unless otherwise stated, all fixtures are wired for electricity by the manufacturer.

A list of suppliers on pp. 174–79 gives the full names, addresses and telephone numbers of the companies cited in the catalog.

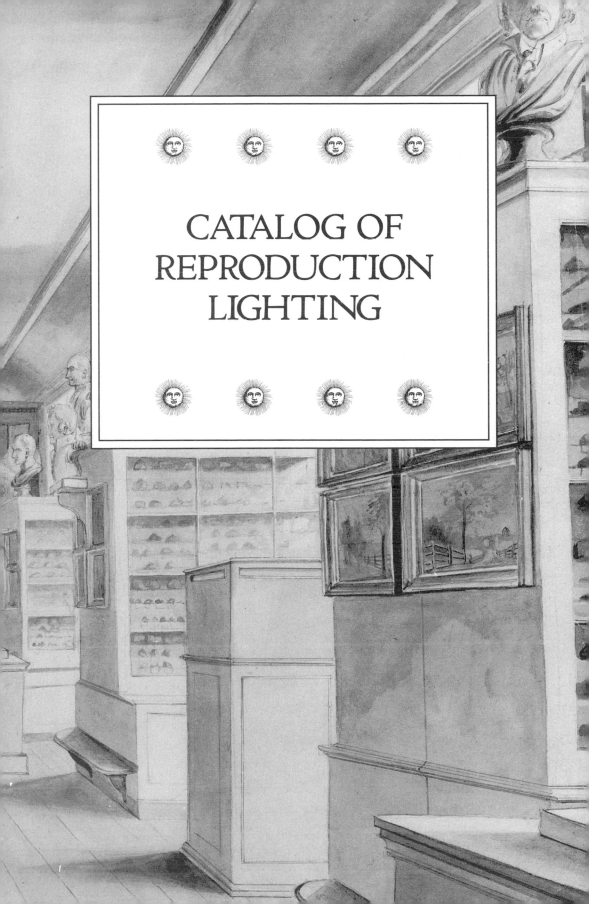

CATALOG OF REPRODUCTION LIGHTING

CANDLEHOLDERS:
1620 TO 1850

The earliest means of artificial lighting involved the management of an open flame: wood, coal or peat confined to a fireplace or stove; a small pool of animal or vegetable fat held by a shallow vessel into which a wick of twisted fiber was thrust; a pithy rushlight of reed soaked in grease to be burned in the jaws of a crude metal holder. All these rudimentary sources of the radiant energy that the eye perceives as light figure in the social history of early American settlements, and even the most primitive lighting devices can be documented in frontier homes well into the 19th century.

Early American lighting is popularly associated with candleholders of all types—simple candlesticks, elaborate candelabra, chandeliers, sconces, lanterns and girandoles. Yet even in the early Victorian era, as Thomas Webster and Mrs. Parkes remind us in their *Encyclopedia of Domestic Economy* (London, 1844, and subsequent editions in England and America), "Candles, from their portability and other qualities, supply, upon the whole, the most convenient and the most general mode of obtaining artificial light for domestic purposes." The Athenaeum of Philadelphia collection contains a pair of cast-brass, gilt-finished, prism-hung chandeliers from the late 1830s that originally were installed in the double parlors of a Philadelphia row house, and another massive, two-tier chandelier, probably by the firm of Cornelius and Company, dating from the 1840s—a period when gaslight was readily available in the city. Gradually, of course, candles were supplanted by gas, kerosene and, ultimately, electricity. But candles remained a popular form of lighting for social occasions, just as they are today.

Man Reading by Candlelight by Rembrandt Peale, c. 1805–08. (Founders Society Director's Fund, Detroit Institute of Arts)

Electrified chandelier, c. 1845–50, hanging in the grand stairway of The Athenaeum of Philadelphia. Probably manufactured by Cornelius and Company, Philadelphia, this fixture replaces a long-lost gaselier of the same period. (The Athenaeum of Philadelphia)

In the decades between 1840 and 1860, such manufacturers as Cornelius and Company and Archer and Warner of Philadelphia, Starr, Fellows and Company and Dietz and Company of New York, and Henry N. Hooper and Company of Boston manufactured thousands of inexpensive girandoles with bas-relief cast bodies, marble bases and glass prisms that were often sold in sets to decorate and illuminate parlor mantels. Intended to be viewed from the front and not in the round, these candleholders were often figured with historic people or literary characters from the tales of popular novelists. Abraham Lincoln's Springfield, Ill., parlor displayed a set of these candleholders in the 1850s, and from the great number that survive in house museums, private collections and antiques shops, they must have been omnipresent in middle-class Victorian parlors.

As coal-gas lighting found its way into American homes, critics such as Clarence Cook in 1881 railed against "monstrous and complicated" gas fixtures and appealed for a return to chandeliers that were "models of

delicacy and grace." "The expense of candles," he continued, "is an item hardly worth considering (it was not their dearness, but the troublesomeness of them that sent them out of use), and every woman knows that no light sets off her complexion, her dress, her ornaments, like the soft light of candles." Nor was electricity warmly received by all critics. As late as 1897 Edith Wharton argued in favor of candles for use in the drawing room and dining room: "Electric light especially, with its harsh white glare, which no expedients have as yet overcome, has taken from our drawing-rooms all air of privacy and distinction," which the soft light of candles helped encourage.

CANDLES. By the time of the first settlements in America, the candle—formed by surrounding a fiber wick with a fuel of tallow or wax—had been in use for centuries. Beeswax provided the most expensive and desirable candles because it burned evenly and required little tending, while bayberry wax—laboriously harvested from the berries of the *Myrica cerifera* shrub—burned almost as slowly and with a pleasant smell. Tallow can-

Set of Rococo Revival girandoles made by Archer and Warner, Philadelphia, signed and dated 1851. (Gift of Samuel J. Dornsife, The Athenaeum of Philadelphia)

dles, however, were made from animal fat, particularly beef and mutton. Because of its low melting point, the common tallow candle was prone to bend or melt in warm weather, attracted rodents, burned rapidly with an unpleasant odor and tended to gutter, requiring constant snuffing to remove the charred end of the wick.

By the mid-18th century, the waxy substance (spermaceti) from the oil in the head of the sperm whale was being used for the best candles. An advertisement from the *Boston News Letter* (March 30, 1748) suggests their appeal:

To be sold on Minot's T. by James Clemens, Sperma Ceti candles, exceeding all others for beauty, sweetness of scent when extinguished; Duration being more than double tallow candles of equal size; Dimension of the flame nearly four times more, emitting a soft, easy, expanding light, bringing the object close to sight, rather than causing the eye to trace after them, as all tallow candles do. One of these candles serves the use and purpose of 3 tallow ones, and upon the whole are much pleasanter and cheaper.

The inevitable decline of the heavily hunted sperm whale in the early 19th century encouraged research leading to the extraction of stearin from animal fats. The resulting soft, white, odorless solid, coupled with the discovery that plaited wicks—as opposed to twisted ones—were less prone to gutter, provided less expensive candles of high quality. It was also discovered that candles with several wicks would give greater light from the same weight of candles because of their efficient combustion; the so-called magnum candles patented by the Englishman William Palmer in the 1830s, for example, had four wicks that were said to last eight hours, required no tending and gave light equal to an Argand-burner oil lamp. Palmer also patented a spring-loaded holder that enclosed the candle in a tube, permitting the efficient use of cheaper tallow candles. Finally, the availability of petroleum in commercial quantities by the 1860s permitted the large-scale manufacture of the modern paraffin candle.

CANDLEHOLDERS. While candles were probably the most common form of lighting in all but the poorest colonial American homes, candleholders of various types were never numerous except in the more prosperous residences. Prints, watercolors and paintings of European and American domestic interiors—documents that are rarely available for any but the wealthiest households—strongly suggest that when not entertaining guests, a family gathered around one or two candles in the evening rather than attempting to illuminate an entire room, a practice that would continue even after the introduction of lamps in the 19th century. Likewise, those parts of the house where the family did not gather—passages and bedchambers, for example—simply were not illuminated. The exception appears to have been the entry passage, where an enclosed lantern typically was provided. When the family retired to bed a candlestick might be available to light the way, although household inventories strongly suggest that candleholders were not commonly kept in bedchambers but rather were collected in the morning and returned to the kitchen or first-floor passage for use the next night.

Travel accounts and diaries provide numerous illustrations of how little light was common away from prosperous urban homes. Listen to landscape architect Frederick Law Olmsted's evocative description of life in a rural household near Petersburg, Va., in 1856. Olmsted had taken temporary lodging with the Newman family, and after dinner he was led to a bedroom.

Brass candlestick, c. 1860, similar to those patented by William Palmer, from Cornelius and Baker, Philadelphia. To avoid "guttering," the enclosed candle was forced against a small opening by a coiled iron spring. (The Athenaeum of Philadelphia)

Mr. Newman asked if I wanted the candle to undress by, I said yes, if he pleased, and waited a moment for him to set it down: as he did not do so I walked towards him, lifting my hand to take it. "No—I'll hold it," he said, and then I perceived that he had no candle-stick, but held the lean little dip in his hand: I remembered also that no candle had been brought into the 'sitting-room,' and that while we were at supper only one candle had stood upon the table, which had been immediately extinguished when we rose, the room being lighted only from the fire. (*A Journey in the Seaboard Slave States.* New York, 1856)

Nina Fletcher Little's pioneering study of 17th-century inventories ("References to Lighting in Colonial Records," *The Rushlight,* March 1941) disclosed that candleholders were relatively rare even in wealthy households. The Rev. Francis Higginson of Salem, Mass., suggested in 1628 that settlers on their way to the New World should equip themselves with a lantern. The estate of John Dillingham of Ipswich, Mass., lists only a lantern hanging by his fireplace in 1636. When wealthy Stephen Gill of York County, Va., died in 1653, his estate included a small lantern and three brass candlesticks in the kitchen.

Wealthier households in the 18th century might have several candleholders for use when entertaining, and typically these would be grouped in the parlor. A random survey of estate inventories of prosperous Philadelphians for the relatively late period 1775–1800, conducted by graduate students in the preservation program at the University of Pennsylvania, disclosed an average of eight candlesticks per household, most of them brass or iron. When silver candleholders were specified, they usually appeared in the parlor, where there might also be candelabra, enamelled sconces or mirrors with branches to catch and reflect the light. A similar survey of rural Bucks County, Pa., households disclosed one or two brass or iron candleholders in parlors and kitchens only, while a survey of 767 Wethersfield, Conn., inventories for the period 1630–1800 and 90 Sturbridge, Mass., inventories for the period 1800–50 yielded the following numbers of lighting devices per household—most of them candleholders:

YEARS	1–3	4–7	8 OR MORE
1650–1700	85%	10%	5%
1700–50	80%	17%	3%
1750–1800	70%	25%	5%
1800–50	64%	29%	7%

Of the 857 inventories examined, 319 listed no lighting devices at all—298 in the earlier survey, 21 in the later. While these are hardly scientific samples, they do suggest that early American households depended primarily on natural illumination—the flickering hearth fire, a smoking oil lamp, the occasional guttering candle or, if it became necessary to venture out in the night, a lantern with its vulnerable flame protected by panes of glass, flattened horn scraped to transparency or decoratively pierced sheets of iron. In the words of Thomas Tusser, the 16th-century English agricultural versifier:

In winter at nine, and in summer at ten
To bed after supper, both maidens and men.
In winter at 5 o'clock servant arise,
In summer at 4 is ever good guise.

BRASS AND GLASS CHANDELIERS. Chandeliers deserve special mention because of their obvious popularity with modern consumers, which is reflected in the large number of reproductions that are available. Both brass and glass chandeliers were imported into America in the 18th century, usually through England. The overwhelming majority of these appear to have been used in churches and public buildings. Students of early lighting believe that the 12-arm brass chandelier acquired from England in 1724 by Boston's Old North Church (1723) is the earliest surviving documented example in America. Like many English and Dutch brass chandeliers of the period, it has a turned center shaft composed of a series of balls and is topped by a cast bird to which the hanger is attached. Shortly thereafter, Trinity Church (1725) in Newport, R.I., acquired its chandeliers, marked "Thomas Drew, Exon, 1728" for an Exeter bell founder. Also in Newport are the mid-18th-century English and Dutch chandeliers at Touro Synagogue (1759–63). Until large-scale American brass foundries developed in the 19th century, cast-brass chandeliers were imported from abroad. Small foundries were producing brass candlesticks, however. In 1782 brass founders James Kip and Richard Leaycraft both advertised in New York City newspapers that they made "a variety of articles in the Foundry way, such as all sorts of . . . Candlesticks, &c."

Most of the English and Irish glass chandeliers that survive in America appear to date from the end of the 18th century or later, although fashionable Virginia Governor Botetourt's 1770 inventory of the palace ballroom in Williamsburg lists glass chandeliers. (Thomas Jefferson had them moved to Richmond in 1780.) It may be misleading, however, to confront visitors to the Pennsyl-

Waterford-type chandelier, c. 1792, from the First Baptist Meeting House, Providence, fitted with wax electric candles. (Stanley Lemons)

vania State House (Independence Hall) with an Irish glass chandelier in the restored Assembly Room. This installation is controversial because there is no documentation for such a fixture in the room about 1776 or, indeed, for any chandelier until one was hung for the celebrations surrounding the Marquis de Lafayette's return for the 50th anniversary of American independence. It is known that the wealthy Philadelphian Thomas Leaming (d. 1797) illuminated his tearoom with a glass chandelier valued at £2.12.6, and there was one in the mansion (1786–88) of John Brown in Providence in the same decade, but such residential references are rare. The Waterford-type glass chandelier at the First Baptist Meeting House (1774–75), Providence, given in memory of Nicholas Brown by his daughter in 1792, survives as an early ecclesiastical example, as does the Venetian glass chandelier now at the Henry Francis du Pont Winterthur Museum presented by Lady Selina Huntingdon to the Prospect Street Church, Newburyport, Mass., in the 1790s.

Glass chandeliers—both imported and manufactured in America—became more common in the early decades of the 19th century, especially in large cities. The English landscape and portrait painter William Winstanley advertised in New York "an elegant pair of large Glass Chandeliers, with furnished gold arms and candle sockets, price 100 dollars" in the late 1790s, and the glass chandeliers now at St. Paul's Chapel (1764–66), New York City, were ordered in 1802. Like most documented examples of that period, the St. Paul's Chapel chandeliers feature swags of glass beads in the neoclassical fashion. In the 1820s George Dummer and Company of New York City announced in the *New York Commercial Advertiser*: "BRILLIANT CHANDELIERS, suitable for Public Rooms and Churches, with four, six, eight, twelve, sixteen, eighteen, twenty four, thirty two, 36 or 48 Lights, for sale by the subscribers; who have also for sale, either at *Wholesale or Retail*, a great variety of Cut and Plain Glass, elegant Tea and Dinner Service;— together with a complete assortment of Earthenware, Glass and China."

EARLY AMERICAN-MADE CANDLEHOLDERS. The 18th-century brass and glass chandeliers known to have been used in America were imported, and most of the widely published examples installed in Colonial Williamsburg—and subsequently reproduced for sale—were acquired abroad in this century. Surviving wood and tinned sheet-iron examples, however, are probably of native manufacture.

Tinned sheet iron itself was not manufactured in America in commercial quantities until after the protectionist McKinley Tariff of 1890. Consequently, the tinned sheet iron used by American whitesmiths had to be imported from heavily capitalized mills such as those in Pontypool, Wales, where iron ore, coal and water power existed in abundance and to which tin could easily be brought by water up the Bristol Channel from Cornwall. Because the American Atlantic seaboard was in regular trade with Bristol, boxes of uniformly sized sheets of Pontypool tinned iron could easily be imported to such cities as Boston, Newport, New York and Philadelphia, where they were purchased by people such as the New York "Tin-Plate Worker," Andrew Coughlan, who fashioned them into "lanthorns and tin speaking trumpets" in the 1770s.

REPRODUCTIONS. Reproductions of these American-made chandeliers, lanterns and sconces—forged from iron, cut, shaped and punched from tinned sheet iron or turned from wood—have been fashioned with traditional tools for several generations in America. Consequently, it is virtually impossible even for the trained eye to detect with certainty whether a particular item dates from 1720, 1820 or 1920. To ameliorate this problem, it seems logical that modern manufacturers catering to owners and curators of historic buildings would turn to the few documented fixtures known to have been used in a particular place in the 18th and 19th centuries or those now in large and carefully studied collections such as Old Sturbridge Village, Colonial Williamsburg, the Henry Ford Museum and the Winterthur Museum.

During the preparation of this book, many manufacturers of these primitive fixtures were interviewed to determine the sources of their designs. The overwhelming majority admitted that they had based their lines on earlier reproductions or on photographs published in books on museum collections. The most popular of these published sources, all listed in the bibliography, are "American Tin Candle Sconces," *Antiques,* August 1936, which reproduces more than 50 sconces then in the collection of Stephen Van Rensselaer; *Colonial Lighting* (1927) by Arthur H. Hayward; two books by Wallace Nutting, *Furniture of the Pilgrim Century* (1921), pp. 554–71, and *Furniture Treasury* (1928), vol. 2, plates 4103–357; and Joseph T. Butler's *Candleholders in America, 1650–1900* (1967).

For the lantern reproductions included in the catalog, those designated as hall lanterns are based on documents intended for fixed interior installations. Portable lantern reproductions, listed separately, retain most of their original portable features, such as carrying handles; occasionally, these might be hung inside. Literally hundreds of available adaptations are loosely based on portable lanterns designed for exterior installation, but most of these have been so modified in scale, material or detail that they are not included here. While most of the portable lanterns listed are wired for electricity, some are designed only for interior use as hall lanterns.

A. J. P., COPPERSMITH AND COMPANY

❋ CHANDELIERS. 16 in a variety of materials and finishes. 18th to 19th century. Adaptations.

AUTHENTIC DESIGNS

❋ CHANDELIER. Turned-wood shaft with 8 curved, patinated brass arms in 1 tier or 12 arms in 2 tiers; fitted for candles or electrified. 18th century. 15½" high, 18½" wide (8 arms); 18½" high, 18½" wide (12 arms). Reproduction of a document in manufacturer's collection. No. CH-101 (8 arms); No. CH-101 2T (12 arms).
❋ CHANDELIER. Turned-wood shaft with 6 curved, patinated brass arms in 1 tier or 12 arms in 2 tiers; fitted

CHANDELIERS

below left
CHANDELIER. No. CH-102. Authentic Designs.

below right
CHANDELIER. No. CH-144. Authentic Designs.

for candles or electrified. 18th century. 21½" high, 21" wide (6 arms); 26½" high, 22" wide (12 arms). Adaptation of a document in manufacturer's collection. No. CH-110 (6 arms); No. CH-102 (12 arms).

✷ CHANDELIER. Simple, patinated brass wheel supporting 12 sconcelike candleholders with reflectors; fitted for candles or electrified. Late 18th to mid-19th century. 20" high, 33" wide. Adaptation. Suitable for a large assembly room. No. CH-144.

BALL AND BALL

✷ CHANDELIER. Turned-brass shaft with 3 or 5 cast-brass arms; S-link hanger; 10" flared glass shades available; fitted for candles or electrified. Late 18th century. 15" high, 28" wide. Adaptation. No. 140-ES3 (electrified, 3 arms, with shades); No. W140-ES5 (electrified, 5 arms, with shades); No. W140-E30 (electrified, 3 arms, without shades); No. W140-E50 (electrified, 5 arms, without shades); No. W140-CS3 (candle, 3 arms, with shades); No. W140-CS5 (candle, 5 arms, with shades); No. W140-C30 (candle, 3 arms, without shades); No. W140-C50 (candle, 5 arms, without shades).

✷ INDEPENDENCE HALL. Turned-brass ball shaft with 7 cast-brass arms in 1 tier; iron chain and hand-forged iron hook; fitted for candles or electrified. Dutch or English, early 18th century. 32" high, 40" wide. Reproduction of the chandelier in the Long Gallery, Pennsylvania State House (Independence Hall), Philadelphia. No. W 135-C70 (candle); No. W 135-E70 (electrified). Special order (3 months).

INDEPENDENCE
HALL. Ball and Ball.

LESTER H. BERRY AND COMPANY

✷ CHANDELIERS. 23 in brass; several finishes; fitted for candles or electrified. Dutch and English, 18th to 19th century.

COLONIAL METALCRAFTERS

✷ LARGE CHANDELIER. Turned ball shaft with 8 arms; solid brass; fitted for candles or electrified. Dutch and English, late 17th to early 18th century. 24" high, 36" wide. Adaptation. No. 216.

✷ 17TH-CENTURY CHANDELIER. Turned ball shaft

with 6 or 12 arms in 2 tiers; solid brass; fitted for candles or electrified. Dutch, late 17th to early 18th century. 17" high, 10" wide (6 arms); 28" high, 26" wide (12 arms). Adaptation. No. 210 (6 arms); No. 212 (12 arms).

ESSEX FORGE

⚙ DEERFIELD. Double-cone center with 4 arms; sheet metal; antique black finish; fitted for candles or electrified. Late 18th or early 19th century. 14" high, 30" wide. Adaptation of a document at Historic Deerfield. Nutting, *Furniture Treasury*, pl. 4144. No. 520.

⚙ NEWFANE. Single-cone center with 6 arms; sheet metal; pewter, antique black, colonial red or bright tin finish; fitted for candles or electrified. Late 18th or early 19th century. 14" high, 30" wide. Adaptation. Nutting, *Furniture Treasury*, pl. 4216. No. 378.

GATES MOORE

⚙ DIAMOND CONE. Double-cone center with 6 or 8 curved metal arms in 1 tier; tinned sheet iron; pewter-coated, painted or distressed tin finish. Late 18th or early 19th century. 11" high, 20" wide (6 arms); 11" high, 23" wide (8 arms). Loose adaptation. Hayward, *Colonial Lighting*, pls. 27, 31. No. 12 (6 arms); No. 12B (8 arms).

⚙ DOUBLEDECKER. Double-cone-over-double-cone center with 12, 15 or 24 arms in 2 tiers; tinned sheet iron; pewter-coated, painted or distressed tin finish. Late 18th or early 19th century. 15" high, 24" wide (12

DIAMOND CONE.
Gates Moore.

43

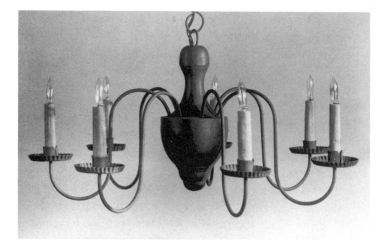

TURNED-WOOD CENTER. No. 2. Gates Moore

arms); 15″ high, 27″ wide (12 arms); 15″ high, 34″ wide (15 arms); 24″ high, 38″ wide (24 arms). Loose adaptation. Hayward, *Colonial Lighting*, pl. 31. No. 12A (12 arms); No. 12 AA (large, 12 arms); No. 12 AAA (15 arms); No. 34 (24 arms).

✪ METROPOLITAN. Metal shaft with 16 curved metal arms in 2 tiers; painted finishes. Late 18th century. 34″ high, 38″ wide. Adaptation of an unusually handsome and complex 18-arm document at the American Wing, Metropolitan Museum of Art. Hayward, *Colonial Lighting*, pl. 43. No. 33.

✪ TURNED-WOOD CENTER. Bulbous turned-wood shaft with 5, 7, 8 or 9 curved brass arms in 1 tier; painted or stained finish. Late 18th or early 19th century. 10″ high, 21″ wide (5 arms); 11½″ high, 24″ wide (7 arms); 11½″ high, 28″ wide (8 arms); 13½″ high, 30″ wide (9 arms). Loose adaptations. Butler, *Candleholders in America*, pl. 56. No. 4 (5 arms); No. 2 (7 arms); No. 2A (8 arms); No. 2B (9 arms).

✪ TURNED-WOOD CENTER. Turned-wood shaft with 6 or 9 curved tinned sheet-iron arms in 1 tier; painted finishes. Late 18th or early 19th century. 11½″ high, 25″ wide (6 arms); 13¾″ high, 30″ wide (9 arms). Loose adaptation. Hayward, *Colonial Lighting*, pl. 28. No. 3 (6 arms); No. 3A (9 arms).

✪ TURNED-WOOD CENTER. Turned-wood shaft with 20 curved metal arms in 2 tiers; painted finishes. 18th century. 28″ high, 40″ wide. Adaptation of a 16-arm document at Colonial Williamsburg. Hayward, *Colonial Lighting*, pl. 45. No. 32.

HERITAGE LANTERNS

⊛ CHANDELIERS. 8 in copper, brass, pewter and wood. 18th to 19th century. Adaptations.

HURLEY PATENTEE LIGHTING

⊛ BIRD HOOK. 2 or 4 arms; wrought iron; not electrified. 18th century. 24″ high, 10″ wide. Reproduction of a primitive document said to have been used at Westover, Charles City County, Va. Hayward, *Colonial Lighting*, p. 13. No. CH 114 (2 arms); No. CH 115 (4 arms).

⊛ CATHEDRAL. Turned-wood shaft with 18 curved iron arms in 2 tiers. 18th century. 32″ high, 60″ wide. Adaptation of a document at Old Sturbridge Village. Hayward, *Colonial Lighting*, pl. 20. No. CH 108.

⊛ COLONIAL DIGNITY. Turned-wood shaft with 6 or 8 curved, tinned sheet-iron arms. Late 18th century. 14″ high, 24″ wide. Adaptation of a 6-branch example in Nutting, *Furniture Treasury*, pl. 4278. Resembles 4-branch example, c. 1800, at the Henry Ford Museum. Hayward, *Colonial Lighting*, pl. 28. No. CH 101a (6 arms); No. CH 101 (8 arms).

CATHEDRAL. Hurley Patentee Lighting.

FLOWING FOUNTAIN.
Hurley Patentee
Lighting.

⚙ COUNTRY. Turned-wood shaft with 3 or 5 curved iron arms. 18th century. 11″ high, 14″ wide. Adaptation of a document at Old Sturbridge Village. No. CH 116 (3 arms); No. CH 116a (5 arms).

⚙ FLOWING FOUNTAIN. 10″ curved sheet-iron center plate with 8 or 12 curved, tinned sheet-iron arms. 19th century. 18″ high, 28″ wide (8 arms); 20″ high, 36″ wide (12 arms). Adaptation of a document now at the Winterthur Museum. Nutting, *Furniture Treasury*, pl. 4156. No. CH 126a (8 arms); No. CH 126 (12 arms).

⚙ MASSACHUSETTS TAVERN. Turned-wood shaft with 9 or 12 curved iron arms in 2 tiers, 3-over-6 or 4-over-8. 18th century. 23″ high, 34″ wide (9 arms); 23″ high, 40″ wide (12 arms). Adaptation of a 9-arm document at Old Sturbridge Village. No. CH 127 (9 arms); No. CH 127a (12 arms).

⚙ MEETING HOUSE. Turned-wood shaft with 12 curved iron arms. 19th century. 20″ high, 41″ wide. Reproduction of a Shaker document from New Lebanon, N.Y., in manufacturer's collection. No. CH 119.

⚙ PENDANT LIGHT. 4 arms; wrought iron; not electrified. 18th or 19th century. 16″ high, 12″ wide. Adaptation of a primitive document at Colonial Williamsburg. Hayward, *Colonial Lighting*, pl. 22. No. CH 118.

⚙ PRIMITIVE. Cylindrical, tinned sheet-iron center with 5 curved arms in 1 tier or 9 arms in 2 tiers. 18th century. 14″ high, 20″ wide (1 tier); 19″ high, 26″ wide

(2 tiers). Adaptation of a document at the Winterthur Museum. Hayward, *Colonial Lighting*, pl. 19. No. CH 122 (1 tier); No. CH 104 (2 tiers).

KING'S CHANDELIER COMPANY

⚜ GLASS CHANDELIERS. Numerous fixtures. 18th to 19th century. Adaptations.

LIGHTING BY HAMMERWORKS

⚜ CHANDELIERS. 17 in tinned sheet iron, copper, brass and wood. 18th to 19th century. Adaptations.

PERIOD LIGHTING FIXTURES

⚜ CONE. Double-cone center with 6 or 8 arms; tinned sheet iron; pewter, aged tin or painted finish; fitted for candles or electrified. Late 18th or early 19th century. 11½" high, 17" wide (6 arms); 11½" high, 21½" wide (8 arms). Adaptation. Similar examples in Hayward, *Colonial Lighting*, pl. 27; Nutting, *Furniture Treasury*, pls. 4144 and 4216. No. C102A (6 arms); No. C102 (8 arms).

⚜ DOUBLE TIER. Double cone over double-cone center with 12 iron arms; tinned sheet iron; pewter, aged tin or painted finish; fitted for candles or electrified. 18th century. 16" high, 25" wide. Adaptation. No. C103.

⚜ DOUBLE TIER WOOD-TURNED. Turned-wood shaft with 14 curved iron arms; painted finishes; fitted for candles or electrified. New England, late 18th century. 22" high, 27" wide. Adaptation of a 16-arm document at Colonial Williamsburg. Butler, *Candleholders in America*, pl. 57. No. C106.

⚜ FLAT ARM. Turned-wood shaft with 7 or 8 tinned sheet-iron arms; painted finishes; fitted for candles or electrified. New England, late 18th or early 19th century. 14½" high, 25" wide. Loose adaptation of a document at the Henry Ford Museum. Hayward, *Colonial Lighting*, pl. 28; Nutting, *Furniture of the Pilgrim Century*, p. 560; Nutting, *Furniture Treasury*, pl. 4278. No. C108.

⚜ IRON RING. 6-arm ring of tinned sheet-iron bands with beaded edges; aged tin or painted finish; fitted for candles or electrified. Late 18th or early 19th century. 15½" high, 23" wide. Loose adaptation. Similar exam-

IRON RING. No. C110. Period Lighting Fixtures.

ples at the Henry Ford Museum and Old Sturbridge Village. Hayward, *Colonial Lighting*, pls. 12 and 29. No. C110.

✪ SINGLE-CONE CENTER. Single-cone center with 7, 8, 9 or 10 flat arms; tinned sheet iron; aged tin or painted finish; fitted for candles or electrified. Possibly 18th century. 11½" high, 23½" wide (7 or 8 arms); 13½" high, 30" wide (9 or 10 arms). Adaptation of a 12-arm document in Nutting, *Furniture of the Pilgrim Century*, p. 560; Nutting, *Furniture Treasury*, pl. 4216. No. C111 (7 or 8 arms); No. C111A (9 or 10 arms).

✪ WOOD-TURNED CENTER. Turned-wood shaft with 6, 7 or 8 iron arms; painted finishes; fitted for candles or electrified. Late 18th or early 19th century. 14" high, 21" wide (6 arms); 16" high, 26" wide (7 or 8 arms). No. C104A (6 arms); No. C104 (7 or 8 arms).

✪ WOOD-TURNED CENTER. Turned-wood shaft with 8 or 10 iron arms decorated with small wooden balls; painted finishes; fitted for candles or electrified. Early 19th century. 10½" high, 36" wide (8 arms); 13¾" high, 46" wide (10 arms). Loose adaptation of a 2-tier, 18-arm document painted white, red, yellow and blue green from a Bridgeport, Conn., church, now in the William B. and Mary Arabella Goodwin Collection, Wadsworth Atheneum, Hartford, Conn. Wadsworth Atheneum, *Let There Be Light*, cover. No. C107 (8 arms); No. C107A (10 arms).

above
WOOD-TURNED CEN-
TER. No. C107. Period
Lighting Fixtures.

left
WOOD-TURNED CEN-
TER. No. C109. Period
Lighting Fixtures.

✪ WOOD-TURNED CENTER. Turned-wood shaft with 8 or 9 iron arms; painted finishes; fitted for candles or electrified. Late 18th or early 19th century. 17³⁄₄″ high, 28″ wide. Reproduction of a document at the Antiquarian and Landmark Society of Connecticut; similar example at the Winterthur Museum. Butler, *Candleholders in America*, pl. 56. No. C109.

✪ WOOD-TURNED CENTER. Turned-wood ball shaft with 8 or 9 scroll-shaped iron arms; painted finishes; fitted for candles or electrified. Early to mid-18th century. 16¹⁄₂″ high, 23″ wide (8 arms); 20″ high, 27¹⁄₂″ wide (9 arms). Loose adaptation of a document at Colo-

WOOD-TURNED CEN-
TER. No. C112. Period
Lighting Fixtures.

nial Williamsburg. Hayward, *Colonial Lighting*, pl. 39.
No. C112A (8 arms); No. C112 (9 arms).

⊛ WOOD-TURNED CENTER. Turned-wood ball shaft
terminating in a carved acorn with 7 or 14 curved iron
arms in 1 or 2 tiers; wooden bobeches; painted finishes;
fitted for candles or electrified. English or Dutch, early
to mid-18th century. 20½" high, 21" wide (7 arms, 1
tier); 29" high, 27" wide (14 arms, 2 tiers). Loose adaptation of a brass chandelier. C113A (7 arms); C113 (14
arms).

PRICE GLOVER

⊛ EIGHT ARMS. 8 arms around a gradrooned central
ball shaft surmounted by a dove with outstretched wings;
solid brass; fitted for candles or electrified. English, early
to mid-18th century. 33½" high, 35" wide. Outstanding
reproduction of a privately owned document. No. PGR-
106.

⊛ SIX ARMS. Turned shaft with 6 arms; solid brass;
fitted for candles or electrified. English, mid-18th century. 21" high, 30" wide. Reproduction of a document in
manufacturer's collection. No. PGR-105.

THE RENOVATOR'S SUPPLY

⊛ CHANDELIERS. 7 in solid brass, ceramic or tinned
sheet iron. 18th to 19th century. Adaptations.

THE SALT BOX

⚙ CHANDELIERS. 7 in tinned sheet iron and brass. 18th to 19th century. Adaptations.

WILLIAM SPENCER

⚙ CHANDELIERS. Numerous fixtures in brass and tinned sheet iron. 18th to 19th century. Adaptations.

VIRGINIA METALCRAFTERS

⚙ APOTHECARY SHOP. 5 or 6 arms; solid brass; polished or antique finish; fitted for candles or electrified. Dutch, early 18th century. 18″ high, 19″ wide. Licensed reproduction of a 6-arm document at Colonial Williamsburg (accession no. 1950:296). No. CW 12894.

⚙ CAMPBELL'S TAVERN. Turned-wood shaft with 8 steel arms in 1 tier or 16 arms in 2 tiers. New England, late 18th century. 18″ high, 23″ wide (8 arms); 26″ high, 30″ wide (16 arms). Licensed adaptation and reproduction of a pair of 16-arm documents painted dark brown and gilt at Colonial Williamsburg (accession no. 1955:325). Butler, *Candleholders in America*, pl. 57. No. CW 12601 (8 arms); CW 12600 (16 arms).

⚙ CAPITOL. 12 arms; polished solid brass; fitted for candles or electrified. Dutch, c. 1690–1730. 24″ high, 26″ wide. Licensed reproduction of a document at Colo-

above left
EIGHT ARMS. Price Glover.

above right
APOTHECARY SHOP. Virginia Metalcrafters.

51

nial Williamsburg (accession no. 1967:705). No. CW 12596.

✿ FLEMISH. 6 arms; solid brass; polished or antique finish. Dutch, early 18th century. 27" high, 25" wide. Adaptation. No. 2100.

✿ NEWPORT. 6 arms; solid brass; polished or antique finish; fitted for candles or electrified. Late 18th century. 37" high, 25" wide. Licensed adaptation for Historic Newport. No. N 2110.

✿ PRINTING OFFICE. 4, 5 or 6 arms; sheet steel; antique tin or black finish; fitted for candles or electrified. Late 18th or early 19th century. 15" high, 26½" wide. Licensed reproduction and adaptations of a 6-arm tin document at Colonial Williamsburg (accession no. 1940:212). No. CW 12579.

✿ RALEIGH TAVERN BAR. 4, 5, 6 or 8 arms; sheet steel; antique tin or black finish; fitted for candles or electrified. 18th century. 11½" high, 27" wide. Licensed adaptation of an 8-arm fixture created for the Raleigh Tavern restoration, Colonial Williamsburg, probably based on a sketch by Nutting, *Furniture of the Pilgrim Century*, p. 561. No. CW 12578.

✿ ROYAL PALACE. 8 arms; solid brass; polished or antique finish. Dutch, early 18th century. 23" high, 40" wide. Adaptation. No. 2150.

✿ TIN. 6 arms; sheet steel; antique tin or black finish; fitted for candles or electrified. c. 1790–1820. 27" wide, 24" high. Licensed reproduction of a document that may have been painted gold at Colonial Williamsburg (accession no. 1960:183). Butler, *Candleholders in America*, pl. 60. No. CW 12580.

LT. MOSES WILLARD

✿ BREWTON. Turned-wood center with 4, 5 or 8 brass arms in 1 tier or 12 arms in 2 tiers, 4-over-8, and bobeches. c. 1800. 10" high, 18" wide (4 arms); 12" high, 20" wide (5 arms); 14" high, 24" wide (8 arms); 21" high, 27" wide (12 arms). Licensed adaptation for Historic Charleston Reproductions. Center turning in Hayward, *Colonial Lighting*, pl. 28. Fixtures of this type usually have wrought-iron or flat, tinned sheet-iron arms.

No. 50091 (4 arms); No. 50121 (5 arms); No. 50101 (8 arms); No. 50111 (12 arms).

⚙ CHANDELIERS. Numerous fixtures in a variety of materials and finishes; fitted for candles or electrified. 18th to 19th century. Adaptations.

BALL AND BALL

⚙ DANA HOUSE. Blown glass and cast brass with smoke bell; amber or clear glass; fitted for candle or electrified. New England. 19½" high, 8½" wide. Reproduction of a document from the Dana House (1807), Woodstock, Vt. No. W-152.

⚙ HURRICANE LANTERN. Blown glass and cast brass with smoke bell; 1 or 3 lights. English, late 18th century. 25"–29" high, 8½"–12" wide. Adaptation. No. W-151 A (1 light); No. W-151 L (3 lights).

⚙ PEAR-SHAPED LANTERN. Blown glass and cast brass with smoke bell; 1 or 3 lights. English, late 18th century. 23"–27" high, 8½"–12" wide. Adaptation. No. W-150 A (1 light); No. W-150 L (3 lights).

LESTER H. BERRY AND COMPANY

⚙ LANTERNS. 6 in glass and brass with smoke bells. Late 18th to early 19th century.

HALL LANTERNS

DANA HOUSE. Amber (left) and clear (right). Ball and Ball.

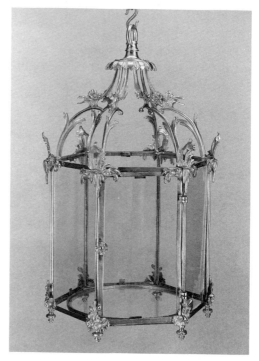

above left
HANGING LANTERN.
No. PGR-108. Price
Glover.

above right
HEXAGONAL LAN-
TERN. No. PGR-100.
Price Glover.

COLONIAL METALCRAFTERS

✪ HANGING SMOKE BELLS. Blown glass and cast brass with smoke bell; 3 lights. English, late 18th or early 19th century. 22″ high, 9″ wide; 32″ high, 11″ wide. Adaptations. No. 230 (small); No. 230L (large).

PRICE GLOVER

✪ HANGING LANTERN. Blown glass and cast brass with smoke bell; fitted for candle or electrified. English, late 18th or early 19th century. 22″ high, 8½″ wide; 27″ high, 12″ wide. Adaptation and reproduction of a document in manufacturer's collection. No. PGR-107 (small); No. PGR-108 (large).

✪ HEXAGONAL LANTERN. Hexagonal; glass and brass with superlative rococo castings; fitted for candle or electrified. English, mid-18th century. 22″ high, 12½″ wide. Reproduction of a document in manufacturer's collection. Similar to "Lanthorns for Halls or Staircases," plate CLII (A), Thomas Chippendale, *The Gentleman and Cabinet-maker's Director*, 3rd ed. London, 1762. No. PGR-100.

THE SALT BOX

⊛ LANTERNS. Numerous fixtures in glass and brass. 18th to 19th century. Adaptations.

WILLIAM SPENCER

⊛ LANTERNS. Numerous fixtures in glass and brass including handcut glass in neoclassical patterns. Late 18th to early 19th century. Adaptations.

VIRGINIA METALCRAFTERS

⊛ BRUSH-EVERARD. Rectangular; glass and solid brass; polished or antique finish; 3 or 4 lights. c. 1775–1800. 18" high, 7½" wide (3 lights); 23" high, 10½" wide (4 lights). Licensed adaptation and reproduction of a 4-light document at Colonial Williamsburg (accession no. 1947:267). No. CW 11751 S (3 lights); No. CW 11751 (4 lights).

⊛ GOVERNOR'S PALACE HALL LANTERN. Hexagonal; glass and solid brass with small leaf finials; polished or antique finish; 4 lights. 18th century. 32" high, 12½"

below left
GOVERNOR'S PALACE LANTERN. Virginia Metalcrafters.

below right
TAYLOE HOUSE. Virginia Metalcrafters.

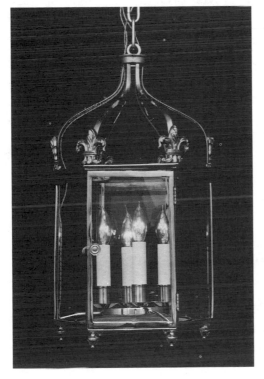

wide. Licensed adaptation of a 3-light document at Colonial Williamsburg that may be a 19th-century revival design (accession no. 1936:159). No. CW 12893.

☼ GOVERNOR'S PALACE LANTERN. Hexagonal; glass and solid brass with fleur-de-lis finials; polished or antique finish; 4 or 6 lights. Early 19th century. 18" high, 20" wide (4 lights); 34" high, 18" wide (6 lights). Licensed adaptation and reproduction of a 6-light document at Colonial Williamsburg (accession no. 1936:573). Could be refitted with an oil lamp for use in the passage of a formal 19th-century building. Webster and Parkes, *Encyclopedia of Domestic Economy*, fig. 145. No. CW 12892S (4 lights); No. CW 12892 (6 lights).

☼ TAYLOE HOUSE. Blown glass and brass with smoke bell; polished or verdigris finish; 3 lights. Late 18th century. 23" high, 10" wide. Licensed adaptation of a fixture created for the Tayloe House restoration, Colonial Williamsburg. No. CW 11758.

☼ WYTHE HOUSE. Blown glass and brass with smoke bell; polished or antique finish; 3 lights. Late 18th century. 23" high, 12" wide. Licensed adaptation of a fixture created for the Wythe House restoration, Colonial Williamsburg. No. CW 12880.

PORTABLE-STYLE LANTERNS

A. J. P., COPPERSMITH AND COMPANY

☼ LANTERNS. Numerous fixtures in copper; variety of finishes. Mid-18th to late 19th century. Adaptations.

COPPER HOUSE

☼ LANTERNS. Numerous fixtures in copper. 18th to 19th century. Adaptations.

JOSIAH R. COPPERSMYTHE

☼ LANTERNS. Numerous fixtures in solid brass and copper; natural brass and copper, antique brass and copper, verde or pewter finish. 18th to 19th century. Adaptations.

HERITAGE LANTERNS

☼ LIBERTY TREE. Hexagonal; glass with freestanding finials resembling leaves; copper, brass or pewter finish; 3 lights; interior ceiling mount. 18th century. 23" high,

LIBERTY TREE. Heritage Lanterns.

10″ wide. Adaptation of 21″ red-painted, tinned sheet-iron documents at Sleepy Hollow Restorations (Historic Hudson Valley) and the Bostonian Society Museum; originals traditionally associated with the Stamp Act demonstrations of 1776. Butler, *Candleholders in America*, pl. 36. No. H385.

HURLEY PATENTEE LIGHTING

✹ PIERCED TIN. Circular with looped handle and cone top; pierced-tin sheet iron; aged tin finish; fitted for candle or electrified; also available without bottom, electrified. c. 19th century. 13″ high, 5″ wide (closed bottom); 16″ high, 5″ wide (open bottom). Adaptation of a privately owned document. Nutting, *Furniture Treasury*, pls.

4268, 4280. No. L122 (closed bottom); No. L122o (open bottom).

⊕ WOOD AND GLASS. Primitive, rectangular; wood and glass; iron wire hanger; fitted for 1, 2 or 3 candles or electrified. 19th century. 15″ high, 7½″ wide, 7½″ deep. Adaptations. Rushlight Club, *Early Lighting: A Pictorial Guide*, pl. 3-65. No. L124a (1 light); No. L124b (2 lights); No. L124c (3 lights).

⊕ WOOD AND PIERCED TIN. Domed with pierced sheet-iron top; wood and glass; iron wire hanger; aged tin finish; fitted for candle or electrified. Late 18th or early 19th century. 10″ high, 6½″ wide, 5½″ deep. Adaptation of a document at the Worcester (Mass.) Historical Society. Hayward, *Colonial Lighting*, pl. 40. No. L121.

LIGHTING BY HAMMERWORKS

⊕ LANTERNS. 16 in brass and copper. 18th to 19th century. Adaptations.

PERIOD LIGHTING FIXTURES

⊕ LANTERN. Rectangular; glass and copper; oxidized copper, natural copper or flat black finish; 1 light; wall mount. 18th century. 16″ high, 5¼″ wide. Adaptation for exterior installation of a common portable lantern. No. L304.

⊕ LANTERN. Rectangular; glass and copper; oxidized copper, natural copper or flat black finish; 1 light; wall mount. 18th century. 16″ high, 5″ wide; 18″ high, 5″ wide. Adaptation for exterior installation of a portable lantern at the Henry Ford Museum. No. L305 (small); No. L305A (large).

⊕ LANTERN. Hexagonal; glass and tinned sheet iron; aged tin or painted finish; 3 lights; interior ceiling mount. 18th century. 19″ high, 8″ wide. Adaptation on a simplified and reduced scale of 21″ red-painted tinned sheet-iron documents at Sleepy Hollow Restorations (Historic Hudson Valley) and the Bostonian Society Museum; originals traditionally associated with the Stamp Act demonstrations of 1766. Butler, *Candleholders in America*, pl. 36. No. L307.

⊕ LANTERN. Rectangular; glass and tinned sheet iron; aged tin or painted finish; 1 light; interior ceiling mount.

c. 1775. 13″ high, 5½″ wide. Simplified adaptation of a document at the Concord (Mass.) Antiquarian Society; traditionally believed to be the lantern that sent Paul Revere on his midnight ride in 1775. Lawrence S. Cooke, ed., *Lighting in America*, p. 123. No. L308.

⊛ LANTERN. Rectangular; glass and tinned sheet iron; aged tin or painted finish; 1 light; interior ceiling mount. 18th century. 16″ high, 5¼″ wide. Adaptation of a document at the Henry Ford Museum. No. L309.

THE RENOVATOR'S SUPPLY

⊛ HALL LANTERNS. 3 in solid brass. 18th to 19th century. Adaptations.

THE SALT BOX

⊛ LANTERNS. Numerous fixtures in glass and brass. 18th to 19th century. Adaptations.

VIRGINIA METALCRAFTERS

⊛ CAMPBELL'S TAVERN. Hexagonal; glass, wood and sheet steel; antique maple or tin finish; 1 light; interior ceiling mount. New England, late 18th or early 19th century. 14″ high, 6½″ wide. Licensed adaptation of a popular portable lantern at Colonial Williamsburg (accession no. 1951:16). No. CW 12700.

⊛ GAOLERS HAND LANTERN. Rectangular with arched top; glass and sheet steel; antique tin finish; fitted for candle or electrified. 18th to 19th century. 14″ high, 6″ wide. Licensed reproduction of a common lantern at Colonial Williamsburg (accession no. 1940:265). No. CW 12800 (candle); No. CW 12801 (electrified).

⊛ SHENANDOAH HANGING LANTERN. Rectangular with polished-brass arched top; glass and solid mahogany; 3 lights; interior ceiling mount. 18th century. 20″ high, 8¾″ wide. Adaptation of a common portable lantern. No. 2120.

⊛ SHENANDOAH TABLE LANTERN. Rectangular with polished-brass arched top; glass and solid mahogany; 1 light; table lamp. 18th century. 13″ high, 5″ wide. Adaptation of a common portable lantern. No. 2121.

⊛ WATCHMAN'S LANTERN. Hexagonal; glass and solid brass; antique brass or tin finish; 2 lights; hall lantern.

Mid- to late 18th century. 21″ high, 9″ wide. Licensed adaptation of a popular portable lantern at Colonial Williamsburg (accession no. 1951:361). No. CW 12921.

E. G. WASHBURNE AND COMPANY

✪ LANTERNS. 6 in solid brass or copper; natural copper, coppertone, antique copper or flat black finish. 18th to 19th century. Adaptations.

WASHINGTON COPPER WORKS

✪ LANTERNS. Numerous fixtures in copper in a variety of finishes. 18th to 19th century. Adaptations.

LT. MOSES WILLARD

✪ LANTERNS. Numerous fixtures in a variety of materials and finishes; fitted for candles or electrified. 18th to 19th century. Adaptations.

SCONCES

A. J. P., COPPERSMITH AND COMPANY

✪ SCONCES. 20 in copper; several finishes; fitted for candles or electrified. 18th and 19th centuries. Adaptations.

AUTHENTIC DESIGNS

✪ SCONCES. 33 in brass; pewter, painted, polished-brass or mottled, blue black gunmetal finish. 18th and 19th centuries. Adaptations.

BALDWIN HARDWARE CORPORATION

✪ SCONCES. 18 in solid brass, some with handblown glass shades; fitted for candles or electrified. 18th to early 19th century. Adaptations.

BALL AND BALL

✪ SCONCE. 1, 2 or 3 arms; cast brass; fitted for candles. English, 18th century. 2¼″ wide, projects 12½″. Reproduction and adaptation of a document in manufacturer's collection. No. W160-C10 (1 arm); No. W160-C20 (2 arms); No. W160-C30 (3 arms).

✪ SCONCE. 1 arm; unusually small; cast brass; fitted for candle. English, 18th century. 3″ high, 2″ wide, projects 5″. Reproduction of a document in manufacturer's collection, probably used originally as a looking-glass arm or branch, as on 2 quillwork sconces with silver arms at the Winterthur Museum. Butler, *Candleholders in America*, pls. 21–22. No. W169-C10.

✪ WOODLANDS. Cast brass; handblown lead crystal shade; fitted for 1 or 2 candles or electrified. 17½" high overall, back plate 7½" high, 3⅛" wide, 10" shade. Back plate reconstructed from a paint shadow discovered at the Woodlands, c. 1790, Philadelphia. No. ES1 (1 light); No. ES2 (2 lights).

LESTER H. BERRY AND COMPANY

✪ SCONCES. Numerous fixtures in brass and glass; fitted for candles or electrified. 18th and 19th centuries. Adaptations.

ESSEX FORGE

✪ CARPENTERS' HALL. Sheet metal and mirrors; aged tin finish; fitted for candle. c. 1774. 17" high, 7½" wide, projects 5½". Adaptation on a reduced scale of the most famous 18th-century American sconce, made for Car-

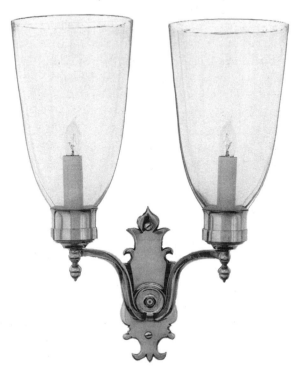

WOODLANDS. Ball and Ball.

CASA AMESTI. Paul
Hanson.

penters' Hall, Philadelphia, site of the First Continental
Congress; based on 24″ sheet-iron documents at Carpenters' Hall and the Western Reserve Historical Society.
Butler, *Candleholders in America*, pl. 37; Charles E. Peterson, "Carpenters' Hall," in *Transactions of the American Philosophical Society* (Philadelphia, 1953), vol. 43, p. 106.

GATES MOORE

✪ SCONCES. 11 in tinned sheet iron; several finishes.
18th and 19th centuries. Adaptations.

PAUL HANSON

✪ CASA AMESTI. Handcut and engraved Venetian mirror back plate; solid-brass mountings; dark old brass
finish; fitted for candle. 14″ high, 6½″ wide. Licensed
reproduction of a Queen Anne–style document at Casa
Amesti, Monterey, Calif., a property of the National
Trust for Historic Preservation. No. T5830.

HERITAGE LANTERNS

✪ CARPENTERS' HALL. Brass or pewter with mirror
back; fitted for candle or electrified. c. 1774. 15″ high,
6½″ wide; 19¾″ high, 8¾″ wide. Adaptation on a
reduced scale of the most famous 18th-century American
sconce, made for Carpenters' Hall, Philadelphia, site of
the First Continental Congress; based on 24″ sheet-iron
documents at Carpenters' Hall and the Western Reserve
Historical Society. Butler, *Candleholders in America*, pl.
37; Charles E. Peterson, "Carpenters' Hall," in *Transactions of the American Philosophical Society* (Philadelphia,
1953), vol. 43, p. 106. No. S540 (small); No. S546
(large).

HURLEY PATENTEE LIGHTING

✪ DIAMOND. Diamond-shaped back plate; tinned
sheet iron; aged tin finish; fitted for candle. Late 18th or
early 19th century. 12″ high, 5″ wide, projects 3″.
Adaptation. *Antiques*, August 1936, p. 59. No. SC308.
✪ DIAMOND DISC. Rare, complex form with clustered
rosettes of leaded tin forming a reflector back plate held
by a glazed wooden frame with a tin finial; aged tin
finish; fitted for candle or electrified. 18th century. 15″

high, 10½" wide, projects 5". Adaptation of a document at the New Paltz (N.Y.) Historical Society. Nutting, *Furniture Treasury*, pl. 4137. No. SC318.

⊕ DIAMOND WITH MIRROR. Diamond-shaped back plate inset with a diamond-shaped mirror; tinned sheet iron; aged tin finish; fitted for candle. Late 18th or early 19th century. 12" high, 5" wide, projects 3". Adaptation. *Antiques,* August 1936, p. 59. No. SC308M.

⊕ EARLY TIN CANDLEHOLDER. Crimped with curved crest; tinned sheet iron; aged tin finish; fitted for candle. 19th century. 12" high, 3" wide, projects 4". Adaptation. *Antiques,* August 1936, p. 59. No. C200.

⊕ FLATBACK. Plain, rectangular tinned sheet-iron back plate with beaded edges; aged tin finish; fitted for candle or electrified. Late 18th or early 19th century. 12" high, 7" wide, projects 3½". Adaptation. *Antiques,* August 1936, p. 59. No. SC330.

⊕ HOODED. Scalloped top; tinned sheet iron; aged tin finish; fitted for 1 or 2 candles or electrified. Late 18th or early 19th century. 18" high, 5" wide, projects 5" (1 light); 18" high, 7½" wide, projects 5" (2 lights). Adaptation of a document in a private collection. No. SC310 (1 light); No. SC309 (2 lights).

⊕ IRON RING DISC. Circular back plate with *repoussé* center surrounded by rosettes of leaded tin to form a reflective surface; aged tin finish; fitted for candle or electrified. Late 18th or early 19th century. 12½" high, 11" wide, projects 5". Adaptation. Nutting, *Furniture Treasury*, pls. 4139–42. No. SC320.

⊕ LANTERN. 3 glass panels and reflector back for wall mounting in passages; tinned sheet iron; aged tin finish; fitted for 1 or 2 candles or electrified. Late 18th or early 19th century. 13" high, 6" wide, projects 4". Adaptation of an unusual lantern. Nutting, *Furniture Treasury*, pl. 4349. No. SC327 (1 light); No. SC327a (2 lights).

⊕ LINED HOLDER. Scrolled top with scored lines defining the tinned sheet-iron back plate; aged tin finish; fitted for candle. Late 18th to early 19th century. 13½" high, 4½" wide, projects 3½". Adaptation of a common design. *Antiques,* August 1936, p. 58. No. C222.

⊕ LINED PLATE SCONCE. Round back plate and incised lines radiating from the center; tinned sheet iron;

above left
IRON RING DISC. Hurley Patentee Lighting.

above right
PINEAPPLE. Hurley Patentee Lighting.

aged tin finish; fitted for candle or electrified. Late 18th or early 19th century. 13″ high, 10″ wide, projects 5″. Adaptation. Nutting, *Furniture Treasury*, pl. 4126. No. SC315.

✪ LITTLE TIN HOLDER. Crimped with round crest; tinned sheet iron; aged tin finish; fitted for candle. Late 18th or early 19th century. 8″ high, 2½″ wide, projects 2″. Adaptation. Hayward, *Colonial Lighting*, pl. 68. No. C207.

✪ LOOKING GLASS. Framed mirror with 2 sconces; tinned sheet iron; aged tin finish; fitted for 2 candles or electrified. c. 1800–25. 20″ high, 12″ wide, projects 8½″. Adaptation of a privately owned document. No. SC324.

✪ MAJESTIC MIRROR. Tinned sheet iron and mirror back; aged tin finish; fitted for candle or electrified. c. 1774. 25″ high, 11½″ wide, projects 7½″. Reproduction to scale of the most famous 18th-century American sconce, made for Carpenters' Hall, Philadelphia, site of the First Continental Congress; based on 24″ sheet-iron documents at Carpenters' Hall and the Western Reserve Historical Society. This is the only copy that retains the

scale and the materials of the original. Butler, *Candle-holders in America*, pl. 37; Charles E. Peterson, "Carpenters' Hall," in *Transactions of the American Philosophical Society* (Philadelphia, 1953), vol. 43, p. 106. No. SC325.

⊛ OVAL MIRROR. Oval back plate with oval mirror; tinned sheet iron; aged tin finish; fitted for candle or electrified. Early 19th century. 16″ high, 9″ wide, projects 4½″. Adaptation. Nutting, *Furniture Treasury*, pl. 4228. No. SC321.

⊛ OVAL PIE PLATE. Oval back plate with crimped edges; tinned sheet iron; aged tin finish; fitted for candle or electrified. 19th century. 12″ high, 8″ wide, projects 4″. Adaptation. *Antiques*, August 1936, p. 58. No. SC305.

⊛ PINEAPPLE. Tinned sheet iron; aged tin finish; fitted for candle or electrified. 1704. 15″ high, 7″ wide, projects 3″. Adaptation of the often-published Hudson River Valley pineapple sconce, originally part of the Stephen Van Rensselaer collection and now at Sleepy Hollow Restorations (Historic Hudson Valley); retains most of the decorative features of the original and reconstructs those that have been lost, with the embossed

above left
MAJESTIC MIRROR. Hurley Patentee Lighting.

above right
PRIMITIVE OVAL. Hurley Patentee Lighting.

"1704" omitted, the candle sockets simplified and the overall scale reduced from 18" high. *Antiques,* August 1936, p. 58; Butler, *Candleholders in America,* pl. 12. No. SC332.

⊗ PRIMITIVE CIRCLES. Concentric-circle back plate with *repoussé* middle; tinned sheet iron; aged tin finish; fitted for candle or electrified. Late 18th to early 19th century. 10" high, 8" wide, projects 3½". Adaptation. *Antiques,* August 1936, p. 58. No. SC311.

⊗ PRIMITIVE OVAL. Oval back with branches; tinned sheet iron; aged tin finish; fitted for 1, 2 or 3 candles or electrified. Early 18th century. 12" high, 12" wide, projects 7" (1 light); 13" high, 10" wide, projects 7" (2 lights); 16" high, 12" wide, projects 7" (3 lights). Adaptation of a pair in Nutting, *Furniture of the Pilgrim Century,* p. 557; possibly based on English or Dutch brass or silver sconces. No. SC301b (1 light); No. SC301a (2 lights); No. SC301 (3 lights).

⊗ RAISED REFLECTOR. Small circular reflector attached to the back plate and a rectangular drip plate with crimped edges; tinned sheet iron; aged tin finish; fitted for 2 candles or electrified. 19th century. 10" high, 8" wide, projects 3". Adaptation of an unusual document. Nutting, *Furniture Treasury,* pl. 4121. No. SC300.

⊗ SCALLOPED FAN. Tinned sheet iron; aged tin finish; fitted for candle or electrified. Late 18th or early 19th century. 12" high, 10" wide, projects 5". Adaptation of a pair of yellow-painted copper French sconces of the same size. Rushlight Club, *Early Lighting: A Pictorial Guide,* pl. 3–53. No. SC313.

⊗ SETTING HEN. Shaped, convex back plate with crimped edges; tinned sheet iron; aged tin finish; fitted for 3 candles or electrified. Late 18th or early 19th century. 11½" high, 10" wide, projects 4". Adaptation. Clarence P. Hornung, *Treasury of American Design* (New York: Harry N. Abrams, 1976), vol. 1, p. 321. No. SC333.

⊗ SOLAR. Large oval back with crimped edges decorated with incised lines and *repoussé* suggesting the solar system; tinned sheet iron; aged tin finish; fitted for 2 candles or electrified. 18th century. 15" high, 9" wide, projects 4½". Adaptation of a privately owned document

SOLAR. Hurley Patentee Lighting.

that may have been inspired by English or Dutch brass or silver sconces. No. SC334.

✪ SUNFLOWER. Round back plate with *repoussé* scalloping around the edge; tinned sheet iron; aged tin finish; fitted for candle. 18th century. 12″ high, 9½″ wide, projects 5″. Adaptation of an unusual pair of documents. Hayward, *Colonial Lighting*, pl. 69. No. SC322.

SUNFLOWER. Hurley Patentee Lighting.

✪ SUNSET. Long oval reflector with incised lines radiating from the center; tinned sheet iron; aged tin finish; fitted for 3 candles or electrified. 18th century. 12″ high, 18″ wide, projects 4″. Adaptation of a design in Nutting, *Furniture of the Pilgrim Century*, p. 557, and a document at the Winterthur Museum; possibly based on English or Dutch brass or silver sconces. No. SC302.

✪ TALL AND SLENDER. Round, crimped top and narrow lines; tinned sheet iron; aged tin finish; fitted for candle or electrified. Late 18th or early 19th century. 12″ high, 3″ wide, projects 3″; 13½″ high, 3″ wide, projects 3″. Adaptation of common documents. *Antiques*, August 1936, p. 58. No. SC335 (small); SC335a (large).

✪ TIN CROWN. Arched top; tinned sheet iron; aged tin finish; fitted for candle. Late 18th or early 19th century. 18″ high, 5″ wide, projects 4″. Adaptation of a document associated with Pennsylvania. *Antiques*, August 1936, p. 58. No. C203.

✪ TULIP TOP HOLDER. Scrolled top; tinned sheet iron; aged tin finish; fitted for candle. Late 18th or early 19th century. 14″ high, 5″ wide, projects 4″. Adaptation. Nutting, *Furniture Treasury*, pl. 4244. No. C204.

PERIOD LIGHTING FIXTURES

✪ SCONCE. Pineapple top; tinned sheet iron; pewter, aged tin, or painted finish; fitted for candle or electrified. Early 18th century. 10″ high, 6″ wide. Adaptation. *Antiques*, August 1936, p. 58. No. S201A.

✪ SCONCE. Curved top with simple, round reflector; tinned sheet iron; pewter, aged tin or painted finish; fitted for candle or electrified. Late 18th or early 19th century. 13″ high, 4″ wide. Adaptation. *Antiques*, August 1936, p. 59. No. S201B.

✪ SCONCE. Crimped cresting; tinned sheet iron; pewter, aged tin or painted finish; fitted for 2 candles or

top
SCONCE. No. S203A.
Period Lighting
Fixtures.

above
SCONCE. No. S203B.
Period Lighting
Fixtures.

electrified. 18th century. 13″ high, 6″ wide. Adaptation of documents at Colonial Williamsburg and Historic Deerfield. No. S201C.

✲ SCONCE. Tinned sheet iron; pewter, aged tin or painted finish; fitted for candle or electrified. Mid-Atlantic region, 19th century. 10″ high, 3½″ wide. Adaptation of a document at the Folk Craft Museum, Witmer, Pa. Elmer L. Smith, *Tinware*, p. 4. No. S201E.

✲ SCONCE. Round reflector back with two rows of tin leaves attached; tinned sheet iron; pewter, aged tin or painted finish; fitted for candle or electrified. New England, 18th century. 11½″ high, 8″ wide. Adaptation. *Antiques*, August 1936, p. 58. No. S202A.

✲ SCONCE. Oval back with crimped edges; tinned sheet iron; pewter, aged tin or painted finish; fitted for candle or electrified. New England, early 19th century. 11″ high, 6¾″ wide. Adaptation. *Antiques*, August 1936, p. 58. No. S202C.

✲ SCONCE. Pointed oval reflector back and crimped edges; tinned sheet iron; pewter, aged tin or painted finish; fitted for candle or electrified. New England, early 19th century. 15″ high, 7″ wide. Adaptation of a document from Sandwich, N.H. Smith, *Tinware*, p. 2. No. S202E.

✲ SCONCE. Tinned sheet iron; pewter, aged tin or painted finish; fitted for candle or electrified. Pennsylvania, 18th century. 11½″ high, 3½″ wide. Adaptation of a document at the Pennsylvania Farm Museum of Landis Valley, Lancaster, Pa. Smith, *Tinware*, p. 2. No. S202F.

✲ SCONCE. Tinned sheet iron and mirror back; pewter, aged tin or painted finish; fitted for candle or electrified. c. 1774. 16″ high, 7″ wide. Adaptation of the most famous 18th-century American sconce, made for Carpenters' Hall, Philadelphia, site of the First Continental Congress; based on 24″ sheet-iron documents at Carpenters' Hall and the Western Reserve Historical Society. Butler, *Candleholders in America*, pl. 37; Charles E. Peterson, "Carpenters' Hall," in *Transactions of the American Philosophical Society* (Philadelphia, 1953), vol. 43, p. 106. No. S203A.

✲ SCONCE. Arched top; tinned sheet iron; pewter, aged tin or painted finish; fitted for 2 candles or electrified. 18th century. 15″ high, 7″ wide. Adaptation of a privately owned pair of documents. No. S203B.

✪ SCONCE. 3 round polished reflectors set into a rectangular back; tinned sheet iron; pewter, aged tin or painted finish; fitted for candle or electrified. Late 18th or early 19th century. 16″ high, 4¾″ wide. Adaptation. Hayward, *Colonial Lighting*, pl. 63. No. S203C.

✪ SCONCE. Oval back; tinned sheet iron; pewter, aged tin or painted finish; fitted for 3 candles or electrified. Dutch, mid-18th century. 14″ high, 9″ wide. Adaptation of a privately owned pair of brass documents. No. S203D.

✪ SCONCES. Round reflector back; tinned sheet iron; pewter, aged tin or painted finish; fitted for 1 or 2 candles or electrified. Late 18th or early 19th century. 12½″ high, 8½″ wide (1 light); 14″ high, 9½″ wide (2 lights). Adaptation of a common document with 1 candle. *Antiques*, August 1936, p. 58; Nutting, *Furniture Treasury*, pl. 4126. No. S203F (1 light); No. S203E (2 lights).

✪ SCONCE. Rectangular back; tinned sheet iron; pewter, aged tin or painted finish; fitted for candle or electrified. Mid-Atlantic region, 19th century. 9½″ high, 4½″ wide. Adaptation of a simple document at the Folk Craft Museum, Witmer, Pa. Smith, *Tinware*, p. 4. No. S204B.

✪ SCONCE. Diamond back; tinned sheet iron; pewter, aged tin or painted finish; fitted for candle or electrified. Late 18th or early 19th century. 8″ high, 5½″ wide. Adaptation. *Antiques*, August 1936, p. 59; Nutting, *Furniture Treasury*, pl. 4241. No. S204E.

✪ SCONCE. Crimped arched top; tinned sheet iron; pewter, aged tin or painted finish; fitted for candle or electrified. Late 18th or early 19th century. 8½″ high, 3″ wide. Adaptation of a common form. *Antiques*, August 1936, p. 58. No. S204H.

✪ SCONCE. Oval; tinned sheet iron; pewter, aged tin or painted finish; fitted for candle or electrified. 19th century. 12½″ high, 6¾″ wide. Adaptation of a simple document at Old Sturbridge Village. Smith, *Tinware*, p. 2. No. S206A.

✪ SCONCE. Crimped round top; tinned sheet iron; pewter, aged tin or painted finish; fitted for candle or electri-

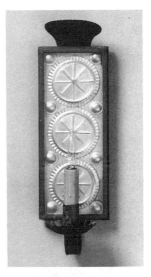

top
SCONCE. No. S203C. Period Lighting Fixtures.

above
SCONCE. No. S203D. Period Lighting Fixtures.

SCONCES. No. S203E (2 lights) and No. S203F (1 light). Period Lighting Fixtures.

fied. Probably 19th century. 11½" high, 3½" wide. Adaptation of a common form. *Antiques,* August 1936, pp. 58–59. No. S206B.

✿ SCONCE. Octagon with crimped edges; tinned sheet iron; pewter, aged tin or painted finish; fitted for candle or electrified. Late 18th century. 11" high, 8" wide. Adaptation of documents thought to be of Pennsylvania origin. *Antiques,* August 1936, p.58; Smith, *Tinware,* p. 3. No. S206C.

✿ SCONCE. Round-back reflectors with radiating ridges; tinned sheet iron; pewter, aged tin or painted finish; fitted for candle or electrified. Probably 18th century. 8½" high, 8" wide; 11" high, 10½" wide. Adaptation. *Antiques,* August 1936, p. 58; Nutting, *Furniture Treasury,* pl. 4126. No. S206D (small); No. S206E (large).

✿ SCONCE. Spiral-crimped round top; tinned sheet iron; pewter, aged tin or painted finish; fitted for candle or electrified. 19th century. 11" high, 4" wide. Adaptation of a common form. *Antiques,* August 1936, p. 59. No. S207A.

✿ SCONCE. Comb back; tinned sheet iron; pewter, aged tin or painted finish; fitted for candle or electrified. Late 18th or early 19th century. 14½" high, 4¼" wide. Adaptation of a type usually associated with Pennsylvania. *Antiques,* August 1936, p. 58; Smith, *Tinware,* p. 3. No. S207B.

✿ SCONCE. Crimped round top; tinned sheet iron; pewter, aged tin or painted finish; fitted for candle or electrified. 19th century. 11" high, 3¼" wide; 14" high, 3¼" wide. Adaptation of a common form. *Antiques,* August 1936, p. 59. No. S207D (small); No. S207E (large).

✿ SCONCE. Stylized pineapple crest; tinned sheet iron; pewter, aged tin or painted finish; fitted for candle or electrified. Pennsylvania, 18th century. 12" high, 4" wide. Adaptation of a document at Lafayette's Headquarters, Valley Forge, Pa. *Antiques,* August 1936, pp. 58–59; Smith, *Tinware,* p. 5. No. S207F.

✿ SCONCE. Oval backs and smaller ovals of sheet mica forming a reflective surface; tinned sheet iron; pewter, aged tin or painted finish; fitted for 1 or 2 candles or electrified. 19th century. 11" high, 7" wide (1 light);

12½" high, 8" wide (2 lights). Adaptation of a document at the Winterthur Museum. No. S208A (1 light); No. S208B (2 lights).

✪ SCONCE. Round back with reflective cut-mirror wedges; tinned sheet iron; pewter, aged tin or painted finish; fitted for 1 or 2 candles or electrified. Late 18th to early 19th century. 11" high, 8¾" wide (1 light); 13½" high, 11" wide (1 light); 12" high, 8¾" wide (1 or 2 lights); 14¾" high, 11" wide (2 lights). Adaptation. *Antiques*, August 1936, p. 58; Nutting, *Furniture Treasury*, pls. 4136–42. No. S208C (1 light, 11"); No. S208F (1 light, 13½"); No. S208D (1 light, 12"); No. S208E (2 lights, 12"); No. S208G (2 lights, 14¾").

✪ SCONCE. Oval back with 3 branches; tinned sheet iron; pewter, aged tin or painted finish; fitted for 3 candles or electrified. Possibly 18th century. 13" high, 9" wide. Adaptation of a large pair in Nutting, *Furniture of the Pilgrim Century*, p. 557; possibly based on English or Dutch brass or silver sconces. No. S209A.

✪ SCONCE. Long with oval reflector; tinned sheet iron; pewter, aged tin or painted finish; fitted for 3 candles or electrified. Possibly 18th century. 10" high, 16½" wide. Adaptation of a design in Nutting, *Furniture of the Pilgrim Century*, p. 557, and a document at the Winterthur Museum; possibly based on English or Dutch brass or silver sconces. No. S209D.

PRICE GLOVER

✪ GEORGIAN. S-scroll brass arm with turned back plate and tulip candle socket. English, mid-18th century. 5" high, 4" wide, projects 10". Wiring available; requires additional back plate to cover electrical box. Reproduction of a document discovered in India and now in manufacturer's collection. No. PGR-101.

✪ NASH TRIPLE ARM. Carved teak shell-shaped back plate with 3 brass arms and engraved, handblown shades; fitted for candles or electrified. c. 1840. 20" high, 19" wide, projects 15". Outstanding reproduction of an early Victorian wall light originally produced by A. J. Nash, Cornhill, London, and now in manufacturer's collection. PGR-110. [See page 23.]

✪ SINGLE, DOUBLE AND TRIPLE ARM. S-scroll brass

arms with blown-glass globes. English, 18th century. 17" high, 6" wide, projects 11" (1 arm); 19½" high, 15½" wide, projects 9" (2 arms); 22" high, 18" wide, projects 10" (3 arms). Wiring available; requires additional back plate to cover electrical box. Reproduction of a document discovered in India and now in manufacturer's collection. No. PGR-102 (1 arm); No. PGR-103 (2 arms); No. PGR-104 (3 arms).

THE SALT BOX

❁ SCONCES. 3 in brass and tin and brass. 18th to 19th century. Adaptations.

WILLIAM SPENCER

❁ SCONCES. 23 in brass and glass; several handcut hurricane shades available. 18th to early 19th century. Adaptations.

VIRGINIA METALCRAFTERS

❁ BRUTON HURRICANE. 2 arms; solid brass; 10" blown-glass globes; fitted for candles or electrified. 18th century. 17" high, 16" wide, projects 9". Licensed adaptation of a document at Colonial Williamsburg. No. CW 16-22D (candles); No. CW 16-22DE (electrified).

❁ BRUTON HURRICANE (LARGE). 1 arm; solid brass; 13" blown-glass globe; fitted for candle or electrified. 18th century. 20" high, projects 10". Licensed reproduction of a document at Colonial Williamsburg. No. CW 16-22L (candle); No. CW 16-22LE (electrified).

❁ BRUTON HURRICANE (SMALL). 1 arm; solid brass; 10" blown-glass globe; fitted for candle or electrified. 18th century. 17" high, projects 10". Licensed adaptation of a document at Colonial Williamsburg. No. CW 16-22S (candle); No. CW 16-22SE (electrified).

❁ CANDLE. 2 arms; solid brass; blown-glass globes; fitted for 2 candles. 18th century. 17" high, 15½" wide, projects 9". Licensed reproduction of a document at Colonial Williamsburg. No. CW 16-23.

❁ PALACE CRIMPED EDGE. Sheet steel; antique tin finish; fitted for candle. 18th or 19th century. 13½" high, 11½" wide, projects 5¼". Licensed reproduction of a document at Colonial Williamsburg. No. CW 13159.

✿ PALACE KITCHEN. Sheet steel; antique tin finish; fitted for candle. Late 18th century. 12" high, 10" wide, projects ⅓". Licensed reproduction of a document at Colonial Williamsburg. No. CW 13158.

✿ PALACE SAUCERBACK. Sheet steel; antique tin finish; fitted for candle. 18th century. 10¾" high, 9¾" wide, projects 5½". Licensed reproduction of a document at Colonial Williamsburg. No. CW 13160.

✿ PALACE WARMING ROOM. Solid brass; fitted for candle or electrified. 18th century. 10¾" high, 4⅛" wide, projects 10". Licensed reproduction of a document at Colonial Williamsburg. No. CW 16-3 (candle); No. CW 16-3E (electrified).

✿ PRINTING OFFICE. Sheet steel; antique tin finish; fitted for candle. 18th century. 13" high, 5¼" high, projects 6". Licensed adaptation of a document at Colonial Williamsburg. No. CW 13163.

✿ REFLECTOR. Sheet steel; antique tin finish; fitted for candle. 12" high, 8" wide, projects 4". Late 18th or early 19th century. Licensed reproduction for the Museum of Early Southern Decorative Arts, Old Salem, N.C. No. OSV5-75.

✿ SERVANTS' QUARTERS. Sheet steel; antique tin finish; fitted for candle or electrified. Late 18th or early 19th century. 10" high, 4½" wide, projects 4¾". Licensed reproduction of a document at Colonial Williamsburg. No. CW 13162 (candle); No. CW 13162E (electrified).

✿ WYTHE HOUSE KITCHEN. Sheet steel; antique tin finish, fitted for candle. Late 18th or early 19th century. 8½" high, 2½" wide, projects 2¾". Licensed reproduction of a document at Colonial Williamsburg. No. CW 13161.

LT. MOSES WILLARD

✿ SCONCES. Numerous fixtures in a variety of materials and finishes; fitted for candles or electrified. 18th and 19th centuries. Adaptations.

WHALE-OIL, LARD-OIL AND BURNING-FLUID FIXTURES: 1783 TO 1859

Two hundred years ago an obscure Swiss scientist living in France found that he needed better light than a candle could provide for his experiments on distillation and fermentation. In solving his problem he unwittingly set into motion a chain of events that to this day affects the way we live. In 1783 François-Pierre Ami Argand (1750–1803) invented the first truly adjustable lighting device, which—despite efforts to patent his invention in England and France—was regarded as a fundamental discovery in universal possession; it was immediately pirated and put into production by manufacturers on both sides of the English Channel.

THE ARGAND BURNER. Argand's invention of the tubular-wick lamp did not escape the notice of Thomas Jefferson, who arrived in Paris the next year. He reported to Charles Thomson in Philadelphia, "There has been a lamp called the Cylinder lamp, lately invented here. It gives a light equal . . . to that of six or eight candles." The Tory exile Benjamin Thompson, who as Count Rumford would give his own name to a lamp, wrote that the illumination from the new invention was so bright that no woman of "decayed beauty" ought ever to expose her face to the direct rays of an Argand lamp. This burner became so fundamental to the technology of lighting in the first half of the 19th century that it deserves detailed description. According to Webster and Parkes in their *Encyclopedia of Domestic Economy* (1844):

Argand, reflecting upon the cause of the imperfect combustion in the interior of the flame of a candle or lamp, and correctly supposing that it was for want of the access of oxygen, conceived the idea of admitting air into the centre of the flame. To

Charles C. Oat's Lamp Store, Philadelphia, c. 1848, featuring a display of solar lamps. (Library Company of Philadelphia)

accomplish this, he made the wick in the form of a hollow cylinder, instead of a solid one as before; and he contrived that a current of air should pass up through this hollow cylinder where the wick was burning, thus admitting air into the middle of the flame. This was found to succeed perfectly on trial: the combustion was more complete, the smoke was diminished, and the brilliancy of the light increased.

Argand also used the fountain feed principle to deliver the fuel (whale or colza oil) to his burner: the oil reservoir was located off to one side of the burner and connected to it by an arm. This system reduced spillage and provided fuel at a steady rate in amounts adequate for extended operation. In addition, Argand and his imitators perfected another feature essential to the burner's efficient operation. As Webster and Parkes explain:

. . . to improve the effect still farther, he also added a glass cylinder or chimney, open at the bottom, surrounding the flame at a small distance, by which another current of air was made to pass upward on the exterior part of the flame, and between it and the glass. Thus every part of the thin circular flame is between two currents of air, which supply the combustion with oxygen so much as to create a heat that is sufficient to consume the smoke and convert it into heat and light.

As Jefferson's letter to Charles Thomson suggests, the chief appeal of Argand's oil-burning lamp was that it provided a brighter, adjustable and relatively clean lighting source to replace the inflexible, messy candles and simple oil lamps then in use for residential lighting. The first Argand lamps arrived in America as gifts from Jefferson, and by the end of the 18th century they had become relatively common in the parlors of wealthy Americans.

The 1800 inventory of Mount Vernon shows that George Washington owned several Argand-burner lamps, and a bill in the Chew family papers suggests that the Argand lamps now in the parlor at Cliveden (1767), a property of the National Trust for Historic Preservation in the Germantown section of Philadelphia, were in place about the same time. Nor are these unique. A random survey of late 18th-century inventories of other Philadelphia houses reveals several examples of such lamps.

One of a pair of double Argand-burner lamps, c. 1820, at Cliveden (1763–67) Philadelphia. (Jack E. Boucher, Historic American Buildings Survey)

Thomas Leaming (d. 1797), whose inventory yielded the early glass chandelier mentioned in the Candleholders chapter, also owned two glass "patent lamps," and the merchant Josiah Twamley, who died the same year, left a pair valued at £7.10 in his drawing room. During the first quarter of the 19th century, lamps were used with increasing frequency, usually in the parlor, together with candlesticks, candelabra and sconces. By the end of this period a single, freestanding astral lamp was common in the parlors of prosperous homes, as were pairs of Argand-burner mantel lamps. The wealthy merchant Lewis Clapier (d. 1837) furnished his small parlor with three mantel lamps valued at $6 and two "branches for candles" valued at $2. His larger parlor contained:

The Lamplight Portrait by Charles Willson Peale, 1822. Here, the sitter, James Peale, reads by the light of an Argand-burner lamp. (Gift of Dexter M. Ferry, Jr., Detroit Institute of Arts)

Two Girandles [sic]	$ 4.00
One chandelier	10.00
Two Mantel Lamps	16.00
Four Branches for Candles	8.00
One Astor [sic] Lamp	5.00

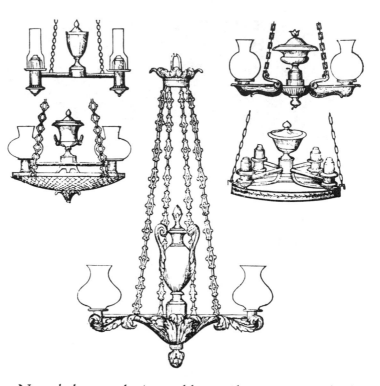

Argand-burner lighting fixtures from Thomas Webster and Mrs. Parkes's *An Encyclopedia of Domestic Economy*, London, 1844. (The Athenaeum of Philadelphia)

Nonetheless, early Argand-burner lamps remained relatively rare because of their cost and the rising price of better grades of whale oil, which they required for efficient operation. In 1841, for example, the wealthy and urbane William Gibbons of Savannah and New York City purchased "1 Cask bleach'd Winter Sperm Oil"—the best grade—for $1.10 per gallon from the New York dealer Samuel Judd's Sons. Between 1827 and 1852 the price of sperm oil rose from 66 cents per gallon to more than $1.50.

ANNULAR LAMPS. By the time the metal burner and filled reservoir of an Argand lamp had been fitted with a glass chimney and shade, the lamp was hardly portable. Later versions of the lamp, such as the tall annular-font astral (starry) and the sinumbra (shadowless), were developed with hollow-ring fuel reservoirs to reduce the shadow cast by the offset reservoir of Argand's early designs. These variations remained stationary features on the center tables of late Grecian-style parlors and are documented by several American prints and paintings that survive from the early 19th century. Here the family

Argand burners illuminating the table of J. Jeater's Subscription Billiard Room, Philadelphia, 1830. (Historical Society of Pennsylvania)

would gather in the evening to read, sew or talk. Surviving examples of these early lamps are so attractive as objects that curators of period rooms occasionally fall into the trap of displaying more examples than would actually have been used.

Smaller Argand-burner lamps could be placed on wall brackets in lieu of candles (as at Cliveden) or fashioned with their own back plates, several burners being served from a single reservoir. By the late 1820s inventories also listed mantel lamps that often came in sets: two single-burner lamps for either end of the fireplace mantel and one with double burners for the middle. As illustrated by Webster and Parkes, Argand lamps could also be made into suspended fixtures with two or more burners. The famous painting *The Dinner Party* (c. 1820) by the Boston artist Henry Sargent illustrates an American use of a suspended Argand-burner fixture: four burners (with chimneys but no shades) supplied from a single font arranged above a shallow glass bowl, not unlike the fixture hung over the first Duke of Wellington's dining room table at Stratfield Saye House, where it can still be seen. And by 1830 Joseph Jeater even illuminated his Philadelphia billiard-parlor table at 40 South Fifth Street with two double-burner Argand lamps suspended from a simple T-shaped fixture that terminated in two glass plates to which the lamps were attached.

SOLAR LAMPS. One disadvantage of the Argand burner was that it required the best grades of oil, which became increasingly expensive as the whale population declined. (The popular European colza, or rape seed, oil, extracted from seeds of the *Brassica napus* plant, was rarely used in America.) Abundantly available lard and lard oil were too viscous to flow easily through the complex Argand-burner mechanism unless first heated and softened.

Throughout the first decades of the 19th century, many more or less successful lamps were patented to burn cheaper lard, lard oil and fish oils. A mid-19th-century broadside issued by the manufacturer Tilton and Sleeper of Fremont, N.H., now in The Athenaeum of Philadelphia collection, trumpets one such lamp:

A NEW AND SUPERIOR LAMP, FOR BURNING LARD. The Patent Adjustable Lard Lamp. This Lamp makes a very economical light, cheaper than Oil or Fluid, is easily adjusted and kept in burning order and will afford more light than any other now in use for the same consumption of burning material. One half pound of Lard will last Sixteen Hours, and give throughout that time a very brilliant light, with no other care than now and then turning the wrench so as [to] force the Lard up against the wick.

Users were directed to:

take a piece of coarse open Cotton Flannel or Drilling the width of the iron slide, put it in double, then unscrew the packing and with a knife fill the cylinder with cold Lard, then adjust the packing on the spiral screw and with the thumb wrench, screw the packing down until the lard comes up to the wick. When a new wick is put in the lamp apply a little lard on the top of the wick before lighting, that the blaze may have some lard to feed upon until the heat melts the lard in the tube. In cold weather, before extinguishing the light, press the lard up to the wick, then it will be ready for use when wanting.

Most of these lamps used flat wicks and pistons or springs to force the fuel into the burner or wires to convey heat from the burner to the congealed contents of the reservoir. Not surprisingly, however, few were fashioned into hanging fixtures for use in parlors or in large public buildings. It was not until the early 1840s that a practical means was found to combine inexpensive lard oil with the efficient combustion of the Argand burner. The resulting solar lamp accomplished this feat by surrounding the burner with a fuel reservoir shaped like a pear balanced on its small end (so the radiant heat of the burner would soften the lard oil) and applying a metal "solar cap" with apertures that forced more oxygen to the flame, thereby reducing the smoke that results from burning cheaper oils while increasing the light to a brilliancy—so its manufacturers claimed—to rival the sun. To reduce the intense glare and to direct the light downward to the work surface, it was not uncommon for solar and other mid-19th-century Argand-burner lamps to be fitted by their owners with paper shades that slipped over the glass shades.

The largest manufacturers of solar lamps in America were Christian Cornelius (Cornelius and Company) and Ellis Archer and Redwood F. Warner (Archer and Warner). Both firms were located in Philadelphia, where they produced a full range of lamps and lighting fixtures in the 1840s. Other manufacturers of substantial size were located in Boston and New York, but the Cornelius firm is especially well known because it was the largest in America and supplied fixtures for the U.S. Capitol, several state capitols and countless public buildings, churches and substantial private homes throughout the country.

With the American population expanding rapidly (from 17,069,453 in 1840 to 31,443,321 in 1860) and new states and towns being founded (seven states admitted to the Union during the same two decades), the demand for lighting fixtures was brisk. By the 1840s and 1850s a well-capitalized manufacturer such as Cornelius could mass-produce interchangeable brass castings and finish, assemble and deliver the completed fixtures to

distant consumers who were erecting large-scale late neo-classical public and private buildings, often in areas where the new gas technology was not yet available. Solar fixtures and lamps with Argand burners adapted to burn inexpensive lard oil were the first mass-produced lighting devices in America.

REPRODUCTIONS OF ARGAND-BURNER FIX-TURES. Regardless of the obvious demand for these handsome and once-popular fixtures, no modern manu-facturer currently reproduces them for use in buildings from the 1840s and 1850s. Nor, unfortunately, is there a single reproduction of a whale-oil Argand-burner fixture that is appropriate for American buildings of the period 1800–40. Because original Argand-burner fixtures dat-ing from about 1800 to 1860 are virtually unavailable in the antiques market (especially in sets suitable for double parlors or large public rooms), the only alternative is to commission custom designs such as those made for Mount Vernon (1743), Andrew Jackson's Hermitage (1831, 1834–36) and San Francisco Plantation (1853–

The Rev. John Atwood and His Family by Henry F. Darby, 1845. A solar lamp is the cen-tral feature. (Museum of Fine Arts, Boston)

opposite
Bedroom of San Fran-cisco Plantation (1853 56), Reserve, La., with custom reproduction solar fixtures produced by Samuel J. Dornsife.

above left and right
Argand-burner chandelier and wall bracket, custom reproductions by Littlewood and Maue for the Willson-Walker House, Lexington, Va.

56). These typically cost several thousand dollars each. The names of firms willing to manufacture custom reproductions are listed on page 162. Fortunately, reproduction chimneys appropriate for Argand burners are available from the suppliers indicated on pages 164–65. Because a glass chimney is essential for the efficient operation of the Argand burner, the absence of a chimney projecting above the shade is an immediate sign that the principles of the lamp's operation have not been understood by those who installed it.

WHALE-OIL AND BURNING-FLUID LAMPS. Small lamps designed to use whale oil or burning fluid are beyond the scope of this book because virtually no electrified reproductions are made, but they deserve to be mentioned because of their use in lieu of candles in late 18th- and early 19th-century hall lanterns. Webster and Parkes tell us that hall lanterns "are either of the vase kind, when small . . . or consist of panes of glass in frames . . . ; and the lights may be, in the first case, simple lamps with one or more wicks, or Argand lamps,

when a stronger light is required. Of course, it is essential that a supply of air shall be given to the light by proper openings in the containing vessel. A glass [smoke bell] is suspended over the lamps, when they are not Argand's, to collect the smoke, which otherwise would blacken the ceiling." Reproductions of glass hall lanterns listed in the previous chapter could easily be modified for use in later interiors by installing a small lamp in place of the usual electrified candles supplied by most manufacturers.

Early whale-oil lamps were manufactured of blown and pressed glass, pewter, brass or tinned sheet iron. The burner fitted into the top of the oil font and held one or two wick tubes about ¼ inch in diameter. (Benjamin Franklin is arguably credited with discovering that two adjacent flames give more than twice the light of a single flame.) To encourage the oil to flow up the wick, whale-oil burners have short wick tubes to bring the flame as close as possible to the font.

Similar in appearance to the whale-oil lamps are those

above left
Solar chandelier by the Rambusch Company for The Hermitage (1831, 1834–36), near Nashville, Tenn. (The Ladies' Hermitage Association)

above right
Argand-burner wall bracket by the Rambusch Company for Mount Vernon (1743), Mount Vernon, Va. The document dates from the 1780s. (The Mount Vernon Ladies' Association of the Union)

Hall lanterns from Thomas Webster and Mrs. Parkes's *An Encyclopedia of Domestic Economy*. The two lanterns on the left are fitted with simple wick (left) and Argand-burner (right) whale-oil lamps. The burning mechanisms are not shown for the two lanterns on the right. (The Athenaeum of Philadelphia)

opposite
Solar lamps and fixtures, hall lanterns, whale-oil and burning-fluid lamps and prism-hung girandoles advertised by Dietz, Brother and Company in *Doggett's Directory*, 1844–45, New York City. (New-York Historical Society)

designed to use burning fluid, which was basically a mixture of turpentine (camphene) and alcohol. As the cost of whale oil increased in the second quarter of the 19th century, American manufacturers sought cheaper fuels that could be burned in these simple lamps. Burning fluid—readily available from the inexhaustible supply of corn and pine trees—offered low viscosity, so it readily flowed up the wick; it also gave a clean, white flame. However, the resulting mixture was so volatile that the lamps were known to explode or burst into flame, and many people were killed or injured by upsetting or dropping burning-fluid lamps. *Godey's Lady's Book* remarked in 1857, "We consider it suicidal to have camphene lamps in a house."

While it was desirable to have the flame of a whale-oil lamp as close to the fuel as possible, wick tubes of burning-fluid burners were taller (1½ to 2 inches) to keep the flame away from the fuel. In addition, to reduce evaporation of the fluid, small caps on chains were typically provided to extinguish the flame and cover the exposed ends of the wicks when the lamp was not lighted. Regardless of its disadvantages, burning fluid was widely used in America throughout the second quarter of the 19th century; by 1857 more than one million gallons a year were manufactured in Philadelphia, selling for 60 cents a gallon. At the same time, the better grade of whale oil was selling for $1.50 per gallon. A few years later the burning-fluid industry was virtually eliminated by the discovery of petroleum wells, and after the Civil War kerosene would become the lighting fuel of choice where gas was not available.

DIETZ, BROTHER & CO.

No. 13 JOHN STREET, NEW-YORK,

AND

62 FULTON STREET, BROOKLYN,

ORIGINAL INVENTORS AND SOLE MANUFACTURERS OF THE

GENUINE DORIC LAMP!

ALSO, MANUFACTURERS AND DEALERS IN

IMPROVED CAMPHENE LAMPS,

Solar Lamps, Girandoles, Hall Lamps and Lanterns,

ASTRAL AND SOLAR SHADES.

CHIMNEYS, AND LAMP GLASSES OF ALL KINDS,

Lamp Wick, Pure Sperm Oil, Camphene and Burning Fluid,

WHOLESALE AND RETAIL, AT LOW PRICES, FOR CASH.

☞ Mechanical and other Lamps repaired; Astral Lamps altered to Solar; Girandoles rëgilt, bronzed, and silvered, &c.

KEROSENE FIXTURES:
1854 TO 1934

Major advances in 19th-century lighting technology can usually be traced to the inventive genius of a few individuals, some of whom—such as François-Pierre Ami Argand—deserve to be remembered for their contributions to the improvement of daily life and work. The discoverers of kerosene are no exception. Two men, the Canadian geologist Abraham Gesner (1797–1864) and the British chemist James Young (1811–83), share the honors.

As early as 1846, Gesner demonstrated that a lamp fuel could be obtained by distilling coal, which he called kerosene. By 1854 he was in New York City, where he patented his discovery and formed the North American Kerosene Gas Light Company. In the meantime, Young began experimenting with the distillation of coal in Manchester, England, where in the late 1840s he discovered a lighting fuel he named "paraffin oil" because of its similarity at low temperatures to paraffin. Young patented his discovery in 1850 and two years later secured an American patent. Both of Young's patents were upheld in England and America, although Gesner's process appears to have resulted in a cleaner fuel. The manufacture of kerosene from bituminous coal and oil shale using Gesner's process began in New York and Boston in the 1850s.

One early advertiser of kerosene claimed that

Pure Coal Oil gives at the same cost
7 times as much light as Burning Fluid
6 times as much light as Sperm Oil
5 times as much light as Lard Oil
3 times as much light as Whale Oil
2 times as much light as Rapeseed Oil
2 times as much light as Rosin Oil
3 times as much light as Candles.

Kerosene task lighting supplementing the gaselier in the apartment of Arthur Dana Wheeler, attorney and prominent resident of Chicago, 1891. (Chicago Historical Society)

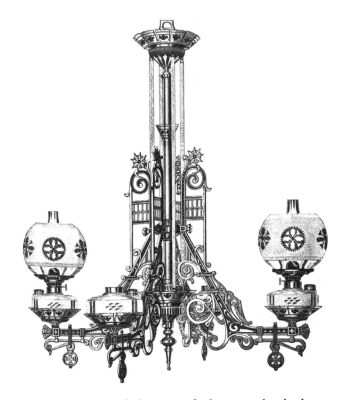

Kerosene "Patent Extension" iron chandelier from the Edward Rorke and Company catalog, c. 1890, New York City. (The Athenaeum of Philadelphia)

Nonetheless, use of the new fuel grew slowly between 1854 and 1859. In the latter year Edwin L. Drake was sent to Titusville, Pa., by the Pennsylvania Rock Oil Company to study the sources of petroleum that had been seeping to the surface. The rest is history. Drake brought in the first drilled oil well on August 27, 1859, and the age of petroleum had begun.

The first oil boom developed quickly, driven by the demand for lighting fuel. In 1859 Philadelphia dealer S. E. Southland, agent for the burner patented by Boston inventor Edward F. Jones the year before, observed:

Kerosene, coal and carbon oils, have already, in a very short time, worked their way into public favor, to an extent scarcely credited by those not conversant with the business. At first imperfect, and exceedingly disagreeable in smell, the oil has at length been DEODORIZED and brought to a state of perfection *hardly anticipated by the most sanguine*. It may now be obtained in any desired quantity and of superior quality. The material for its manufacture is *absolutely inexhaustible*. That it will eventually come into universal use, with all such as desire to *avoid danger*, and at the same time possess themselves of the

Kerosene "Hall Lamps" from the same Rorke catalog. (The Athenaeum of Philadelphia)

very best and MOST ECONOMICAL artificial Light within their reach, there cannot be a doubt.

The rapid construction of Pennsylvania refineries and the ease with which the new lighting fuel could be delivered via the expanding American railroad network (from 3,000 miles in 1840 to 30,626 in 1860) virtually guaranteed that whale oil, burning fluid and even lard oil would be supplanted by kerosene. Burning fluid briefly held its own against kerosene in the late 1850s, but the dramatic increase in the cost of turpentine during the Civil War helped bring about its demise.

KEROSENE LAMPS. In the 10 months between March 1, 1862, and December 30, 1862, 623 patents were granted for petroleum burners and lamps. In addition to kerosene's cost, cleanliness, relative safety and bright light, virtually any lamp or fixture could be converted to burn it. Thousands of whale-oil, burning-fluid and solar lamps were converted simply by removing the old burner (and filling the center-draft intake of an Argand burner) and replacing it with one of the many kerosene flat-wick

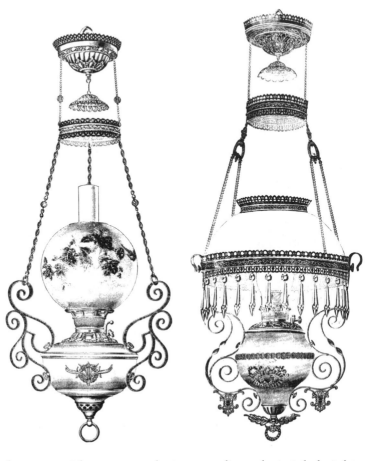

Kerosene "Library Lamps" from the Edward Rorke and Company catalog, c. 1890, New York City. (The Athenaeum of Philadelphia)

burners with a rotary device to adjust the wick height. Virtually any liquid-tight container, regardless of size, material or design, could be adapted as a kerosene lamp.

The conversion required even less effort in the case of solar fixtures with removable fonts. The magnificent Philadelphia Rococo Revival solar chandeliers at Lansdowne (1853) in Natchez, Miss., for example, were converted to kerosene following the Civil War by dropping into the ring at the end of each arm a glass kerosene font, a burner and a chimney of the same diameter as the original brass solar font. Never was an advance in residential lighting so painless as the conversion to kerosene.

In American buildings dependent until then on fuels other than gas, kerosene lamps and fixtures became the dominant lighting technology from the 1860s until well into the 20th century. Even in those buildings where gas

Kerosene wall brackets from the Rorke catalog. (The Athenaeum of Philadelphia)

was available, kerosene replaced whale oil, lard oil and burning fluid for portable table-top task lighting that had always supplemented inflexible gas ceiling fixtures and wall brackets. In rural America, kerosene lighting, often utilizing Welsbach mantles, which gave a bright, efficient light, would remain common until the advent of rural electrification in the 1930s. The ubiquitous kerosene burner still sold today was invented by John Atwood of Waterbury, Conn., in 1873.

The majority of kerosene lighting devices were relatively portable lamps that are, like candlesticks and oil lamps, beyond the scope of this book. Most owners of historic buildings prefer to select appropriate lamps from the seemingly limitless variety offered by dealers in antique lighting. Fabric lamp shades were often used for decoration or to reduce the glare of Welsbach-burner kerosene lamps, and extensive reproductions of these are available for the period 1890–1920 (see pages 163–64).

HANGING LAMPS AND WALL BRACKETS. Kerosene hanging lamps and wall brackets for hallways, libraries and parlors were manufactured for use where gas and, later, electricity were not available. Most of these consist of brass or iron frames to hold the "lamp," which could be easily lifted out and carried to the kitchen, where the chimneys were washed, wicks trimmed and fonts refilled without endangering carpets and upholstery—a daily task in the pre-electrical household. Unfortunately, few modern manufacturers are reproducing kerosene fixtures, preferring to jump over them in favor of gas and gas-electric combination fixtures. As the following items indicate, however, it is possible to acquire simple reproduction ceiling-fixture and wall-bracket frames into which antique kerosene lamps will fit.

HANGING LAMPS

B AND P LAMP SUPPLY

A major wholesaler of tubing, castings, electrical fittings and glass used in assembling light fixtures. Its catalog also offers one of the most extensive lines of assembled kerosene-style fixtures and lamps dating from the 1870s through the early 20th century.

❂ HANGING LAMP. Cast-iron-frame library lamp with handblown opal shade and kerosene font; satin black finish. c. 1880. 28″ high, 10″ wide. No. 63102.

❂ HANGING LAMP. Cast-iron-frame counterweight library lamp with handblown opal shade, kerosene font and smoke bell; satin black finish. c. 1870. 31″ high, 14″ wide. Adaptation of a George H. Lomax patent lamp. Russell, *A Heritage of Light*, pp. 221–23; Thuro, *Oil Lamps*, p. 72. No. 69121.

❂ HANGING LAMP. Cast-brass-frame library lamp with hobnail blue satin-glass shade, polished brass font and frame hung with crystal prisms. c. 1890. 29″ high, 14″ wide. No. 69400.

❂ HANGING LAMP. Cast-brass-frame library lamp with a variety of decorated shades, Classical Revival brass font and frame hung with crystal prisms. c. 1890. 33½″ high, 14″ wide. No. 69402.

HANGING LAMP. No. 69121. B and P Lamp Supply.

⊛ HANGING LAMP. Cast-brass-frame library lamp with a variety of decorated shades, florid cast-brass font featuring cherubim amid roses and frame hung with crystal prisms. c. 1890–1900. 32″ high, 14″ wide. No. 69404.

⊛ HANGING LAMP. Cast-brass-frame library lamp with a variety of decorated shades, polished brass font and frame hung with crystal prisms. c. 1880–90. 33″ high, 14″ wide. No. 69406.

⊛ HANGING LAMP. Cast-brass-frame library lamp with handpainted American Beauty rose shade and font, and frame hung with crystal prisms. c. 1880–90. 33″ high, 14″ wide. Russell, *A Heritage of Light*, pp. 270–73. No. 69408.

✹ HANGING LAMP. Cast-brass-frame library lamp with handpainted shade with violets, polished Colonial Revival font and hanging rods, and frame hung with crystal prisms. c. 1880. 38″ high, 14″ wide. No. 69410.

✹ HANGING LAMP. Cast-brass-frame library lamp with floral-decorated shade and font. c. 1890. 28″ high, 10″ wide. No. 69412.

WINDY LANE FLUORESCENTS

✹ HANGING LAMPS. Brass and brass-finish-frame library lamps with floral-decorated or plain opaline china shades and fonts. c. 1890–1900. Adaptations.

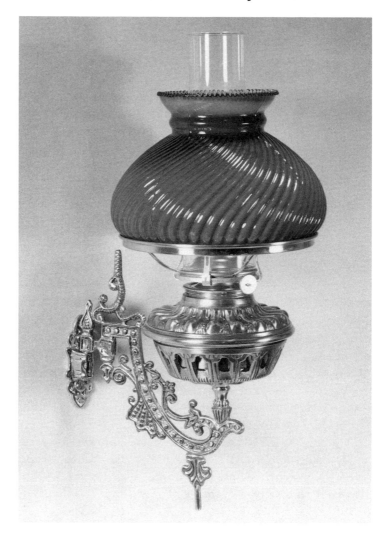

CAST-BRASS WALL BRACKET. No. 10580. B and P Lamp Supply.

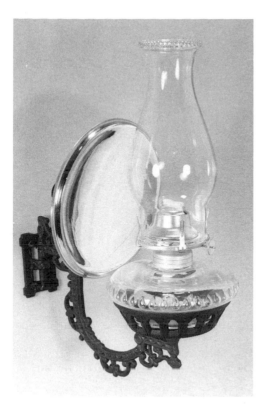

B AND P LAMP SUPPLY

✪ CAST-BRASS WALL BRACKET. Accepts kerosene-style 3½" font; extends 9"; polished and lacquered. c. 1870–90. No. 10580.

✪ CAST-IRON WALL BRACKET. Accepts kerosene-style 5¾" font and 7½" mercury-glass reflector; extends 11", dull black finish. c. 1879–90. No. 73801.

✪ CAST-IRON WALL BRACKET. Accepts kerosene-style 3½" font; extends 11"; dull black finish. c. 1870–90. No. 73803.

✪ CAST-IRON WALL BRACKET. Fluted bowl. Accepts kerosene-style 3¾" font; extends 9"; dull black finish. c. 1870–90. No. 73804.

✪ CAST-IRON WALL BRACKET. Simple gallery bowl. Accepts kerosene-style 3¾" font; extends 9"; dull black finish. c. 1870–90. No. 73805.

✪ DOUBLE CAST-IRON WALL BRACKET. Accepts 2 kerosene-style 3½" fonts; extends 11"; dull black finish. c. 1870–90. No. 73813.

WALL BRACKETS

above left
CAST-IRON WALL BRACKET. No. 73801. The shade (not described here) is No. 63317. B and P Lamp Supply.

above right
CAST-IRON WALL BRACKET. No. 73803. B and P Lamp Supply.

GAS LIGHTING:
1817 TO 1907

By 1860, when kerosene was rapidly gaining favor over whale oil, lard oil and burning fluid, 381 American cities and towns could already boast of gas generating plants—337 in the North and 44 in the more rural South. Even though it was estimated in December 1859 that 22,750 gallons of kerosene were being manufactured daily, the older gas technology continued to dominate in those cities with gas plants, especially for street lighting and for use in large commercial and public buildings.

The use of manufactured coal gas as an illuminant had been known in Europe since the 17th century. It was Philippe Lebon of France, however, who obtained the first patent in 1799. The Englishman William Murdoch installed gas lighting in a London factory in 1798, and by 1810 the Moravian Frederic Albert Winzer (anglicized to Winsor) had patented a successful manufacturing process, formed a company and installed the first gas street lighting system in London.

Philadelphia led the way in the earliest demonstrations of gas in America when the Italian fireworks manufacturer M. Ambroise and Company exhibited lights arranged in the form of figures, temples and Masonic devices in August 1796, although Baltimore deserves the credit for authorizing in 1816 the first gas street lighting system, which went into operation on February 7, 1817. In spite of Thomas Cooper's urging in *Some Information Concerning Gas Lights* (Philadelphia, 1816), Philadelphia did not charter a gas company until 1835, and it got under way February 8, 1836, long after similar companies had been chartered in Boston and New York.

FLORA. Nowell's. (See page 116.)

THE MANUFACTURE OF GAS. While scattered references to the use of natural gas for lighting can be found in the 19th century, early illuminating gas was manufactured mostly from bituminous coal. This was accomplished by heating the coal in a retort; as it decomposed, hydrocarbons (methane, ethylene, acetylene) and such undesirable products as volatile liquids, tar, ammonia, hydrogen sulphide and carbon dioxide were released. The latter byproducts had to be removed with condensers, scrubbers and filters. According to one author, "The purification of the gas demands the utmost vigilance on the part of those who superintend gas-works, and is the part of gas-making with which the public is chiefly concerned: an ill-conducted gas-work affords not only an imperfect light, but emits offensive and deleterious effluvia." (Not surprisingly, therefore, the area of a city near the gasworks became undesirable.) Once purified, the gas passed into a gasometer, where it was trapped until drawn off by pipe to be burned. Each coal-gas burner gave a light equal to 15 to 17 candlepower. After 1872 coal gas was supplanted by hydrogen-rich water gas generated by superheated steam and anthracite coal or petroleum, and by 1890 most of the 742 American gasworks had been converted to the more efficient system. A single home burner using water gas and a Welsbach burner provided light equal to 22 to 35 candlepower.

Portable gas systems made it possible for commercial establishments and large private residences to have gas beyond the range of municipal gasworks. The popular Springfield Gas Machine, for example, generated lighting gas from gasoline in the 1860s. The generator was placed under ground away from the building—for obvious reasons—and an air pump in the basement circulated the gas into the pipes that supplied the fixtures.

GAS FIXTURES. Introduced originally for lighting streets, factories, commercial establishments and public buildings, gas did not find immediate favor for residential use. Edgar Allen Poe complained in 1840 that it was "totally inadmissable within doors. Its harsh and unsteady light offends. No one having both brains and eyes will use it." And Fredrika Bremer wrote in 1850, "Evening parties do not agree with me; the heat produced by the gas-lights

of the drawing-rooms makes me feverish." Such objections notwithstanding, gas gradually found its way into city houses in the 1840s and 1850s as scrubbers and filters reduced disagreeable smells and removed impurities that caused early burners to smoke.

A typical residential gas installation would include gas chandeliers (called gaseliers by the 1840s) with several burners hanging from the ceiling of the principal rooms; wall brackets, often placed on either side of windows, where they became a common cause of curtain fires; lanterns or pendants in passageways, vestibules and stairwells; and newel-post lights at the foot of the main stair. The cost of installation and the inflexibility of gas pipes were the main objections to gas lighting once ways had been found to remove the impurities. Gas mains had to be buried under the streets and installed in building walls. In existing buildings, consequently, many gas installations were rudimentary affairs, but as the mains spread throughout American cities, new buildings were provided with piping to supply wall and ceiling fixtures.

Country mansion, with a Springfield Gas Machine (left foreground), 1872, designed "especially for lighting isolated buildings, or those situated beyond the reach of the coal gas mains of cities." (The Athenaeum of Philadelphia)

Gaseliers, a wall bracket and a table lamp from the Oxley, Giddings and Enos Company catalog, c. 1890–1900, New York City. (The Athenaeum of Philadelphia)

The decorative style of a gas fixture is, of course, incidental to its purpose. A pipe delivers the gas to a burner with an adjustable gas cock to regulate the flow. There are infinite variations of these burners, although they classify roughly into five main types: ratstail, batswing, fishtail (names that refer to the shape of the flame they produce), the Argand (operating on the center-draft principle described in an earlier chapter) and the Welsbach burner. The latter was invented about 1885 by the Austrian chemist Carl Auer von Welsbach and operates like a Bunsen burner to heat to incandescence a cotton-gauze mantle impregnated with rare earth oxides. The Welsbach burner, according to one account, "gives out a brilliant, mellow light, which it may be said, without any exaggeration, will compare favorably with any electric light yet put on the market." Coupled with water gas, the Welsbach burner gave the gas lighting industry a new lease on life. Not only did the Welsbach burner give a brighter light than the early carbon-filament electric bulbs, it also was more reliable. If the gas industry had not developed these improvements at the same time electricity was introduced, it is likely that electric lighting for residential structures would have spread more rapidly.

Gas lighting tended to make the arrangement of furniture more static in the Victorian age. Where previously furniture might be arranged around the walls and then moved as needed to take advantage of natural light, the inflexibility of gas discouraged this practice, just as the need to protect upholstery, carpets and window treatments from the harmful effects of the sun increasingly favored interior shutters, window shades and heavier curtaining. The home was turning its back on natural illumination for the first time. In the parlor, the library and, especially, the dining room, gaseliers were commonly equipped with counterbalances that allowed the fixtures to be lowered over a table in the center of the room. (In the mid-19th century, crystal gaseliers were usually used in the parlor, not in the dining room.) Gaseliers were also provided with an extra gas cock to which a flexible hose could be attached (not unlike an electric extension cord) to supply a table lamp. As Webster and Parkes tell us:

Gas lamps may, to a certain extent, be made portable, by having a flexible tube of caoutchouc [India rubber or gum elastic, as it was known in the 19th century] coming from the service gas pipe, and reaching to the place where the gas is required to burn, where it may supply a stand like that of an ordinary candlestick or lamp. This stand may be detached when required, by having one cock at the service pipe, and another at the stand. These are found useful for the desk in offices or other places lighted with gas.

Nonetheless, photographs of post–Civil War interiors suggest that kerosene lamps were also used for portable and table-top task lighting.

Gas fixtures' low levels of light—by modern standards—should suggest to architects, curators and homeowners that the illumination provided by 40- to 100-watt bulbs for which most reproductions are typically wired will be unhistorical. The alternatives are to install low-voltage transformers or individual fixture dimmers or to change the electrical sockets to accept small, candle-socket lamps of the 10- to 15-watt size. It is also

103

desirable to disguise the electrical socket sleeve by painting it dark gray or black.

REPRODUCTIONS. Reproductions of mid-19th-century gas chandeliers are not common among manufacturers today because the initial investment for molds, castings, finishing and shades is so high. In a market where annual sales of 100 to 200 units of an expensive fixture are considered satisfactory, the recovery time on the investment may be several years. Also, the typical 2½-inch fitter shades (handcut in appropriate patterns) are not readily available from domestic glass houses. Regardless of these problems, large-volume manufacturers are gradually responding to the demand for documented reproductions from this period. In this market, Progress Lighting has a temporary lead.

Gaseliers dating from the last quarter of the 19th century generally require fewer custom castings than those based on mid-19th-century documents and consequently are less likely to be reproduced as a unit from a single document. Like late Victorian manufacturers, the leading modern firms in this field use various castings, die-stamped frames and bent tubing interchangeably to create different combinations. Rather than being taken from a single document, the elements prove on examination to be from an assortment selected by the manufacturer because they were pleasing and available: an arm from one, the gas cock from another. Most of these fixtures are loosely based on originals owned by the manufacturers or worked on when they specialized in restoring fixtures; many of the manufacturers of Victorian lighting began by restoring original fixtures and gradually moved into reproductions. But because the elements used by these manufacturers derive stylistically from colonial, classical or exotic revivals and Art Nouveau designs, the resulting fixtures often defy stylistic classification. This eclecticism was characteristic of late 19th- and early 20th-century fixtures as well. Many firms in this field also assemble less expensive fixtures from elements acquired through wholesale jobbers; at best, these can be called adaptations that capture the spirit of the originals. They are listed accordingly in groups rather than individually.

Some reproductions of turn-of-the-century hall lights, pendants and lanterns—generally narrow fixtures intended for use in hallways, entries and kitchens—are available. They should be hung at the same 78-to-84-inch height from the floor recommended for parlor gaseliers, although it may be necessary to go somewhat higher in narrow vestibules if the in-swinging doors are exceptionally tall.

Newel-post fixtures were so common in the last quarter of the 19th century that it is unfortunate that so few manufacturers reproduce them. Often these fixtures were castings of figures from classical mythology or famous persons such as Christopher Columbus; probably the cost of such castings has frightened away today's manufacturers. This should change as more late 19th-century houses are restored and homeowners seek these attractive and useful fixtures.

Gas-style wall brackets appropriate for the years 1850–90, like gaseliers from the same period, are rarely reproduced because of the high initial cost of the castings; later fixtures can be simulated more readily with small castings and bent tubing. While most of the cast brackets listed in the catalog are reproduced from examples of the 1870s and later, they are acceptable in buildings from the previous decade, especially if they are refitted to take shades with 2½-inch bases rather than the wider, and later, 4-inch size, which is the standard fitting for most manufacturers.

PROGRESS LIGHTING

⊛ CLASSICAL. 4 brass arms with 4 tiers of lead crystal prisms; Greek-key-design etched shades. 1840s. 29″ wide, min. length 35″, max. length 48″, 2½″ shade fitters. Reproduction of a document attributed to Cornelius and Company at The Athenaeum of Philadelphia. No. P-4048.

⊛ ROCOCO. 4 solid cast-brass arms with leafy vine and grape cluster brass chains; grape-leaf-design etched shades. 1850s. 29″ wide, min. length 40″, max. length 51″, 2½″ shade fitters. Reproduction of a document attributed to Archer and Warner at The Athenaeum of Philadelphia. No. P-4063. [Illustrated on the cover.]

CLASSICAL. Progress Lighting.

CHARLESTON. King's Chandelier Company.

GASELIERS: LATE 19TH CENTURY

CLASSIC ILLUMINATION

❂ GASELIER. 2, 3, 4, 5 or 6 arms; several finishes. Late 19th century. 30″ wide, various lengths, 4″ shade fitters. Adaptation of several documents. No. 1800.

❂ GRIFFIN. 2, 3, 4, 5 or 6 griffin-style arms; 3 finishes. Late 19th century. 30″ wide, various lengths, 4″ shade fitters. Adaptation of an 1870s privately owned document, assembled in a late 19th-century form with later 4″ shade fitters; uses the same arm casting as Classic Illumination gas wall bracket no. 1875-1. No. 1870.

D'LIGHTS

❂ GASELIERS. 4 in brass. Turn-of-the-century look. Not based on specific documents.

KING'S CHANDELIER COMPANY

❂ CHARLESTON. Crystal with 5, 6, 8 or 12 rope-turned brass arms hung with notched spear-point prisms and 18 strands of graduated crystal buttons. Mid-19th century. 25″–38″ wide, 29″–40″ long, 4″ shade fitters. Fitted for a chain; correct mounting requires a gas pipe. Adaptation.

GRIFFIN. Classic Illumination.

M-H LAMP AND FAN COMPANY

✪ GAS-STYLE CHANDELIERS. 3 in brass with 4, 5 or 6 arms. Turn-of-the-century look. Not based on specific documents.

NOWELL'S

✪ CAESAR'S GRILL. Classical Revival center with 3 gracefully curved arms; antique or polished brass finish. Late 19th century. 28″ wide, min. length 24″, max.

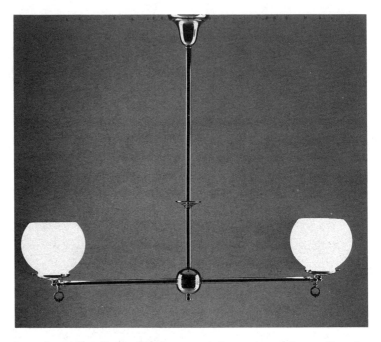

MEIGGS WHARF.
Nowell's.

length 42″, 4″ shade fitters. Adaptation of a privately owned document in San Francisco.

⚙ EMBARCADERO. 12 arms in 2 tiers; antique or polished brass finish. Turn of the century. 70″ wide, min. length 54″, max. length 60″, 4″ shade fitters. Loose adaptation of Colonial Revival documents.

⚙ LUCKY BALDWIN. Classical Revival reeded urn center with 3 arms; antique or polished brass finish. 28″ wide, min. length 24″, max. length 42″, 4″ shade fitters.

⚙ MEIGGS WHARF. Simple 2-arm T-shaped fixture; antique or polished brass finish. Turn of the century. 40″ wide, min. length 21″, max. length 40″, 4″ shade fitters. Adaptation of a store pendant from the J. B. Colt catalog. Suitable for residential hallways and stair landings and public buildings where more ornate fixtures would be inappropriate.

⚙ NOB HILL. Classical Revival with 12 arms in 2 tiers; antique or polished brass finish. Turn of the century. 36″ wide, min. length 42″, max. length 60″, 4″ shade fitters. Adaptation of a privately owned document in San Francisco. Also available: "Telegraph Hill." 8 arms in 1 tier. "Potrero Hill." 16 arms in 3 tiers.

✪ SILVER PALACE. Classical Revival reeded urn with 4 arms; antique or polished brass finish. 28″ wide, min. length 24″, max. length 42″, 4″ shade fitters.

✪ VAN NESS. 6 arms; antique or polished brass finish. Late 19th century. 41″ wide, min. length 36″, max. length 60″, 4″ shade fitters. Adaptation of a document at the Parrot House, Saint Helena, Calif.

PROGRESS LIGHTING

✪ ART NOUVEAU. Flowering dogwood design with 2 or 4 arms and ribbed shades. c. 1900. 26″ wide, min. length 19″, max. length 44″, 4″ shade fitters. Reproduction from a catalog of the Gibson Fixture Works, Philadelphia, at The Athenaeum of Philadelphia. No. P-3607 (2 arms); No. P-4041 (4 arms). [Illustrated on p. 25.]

REJUVENATION LAMP AND FIXTURE COMPANY

✪ KING'S HILL. Classical Revival reeded center with 3, 4, 5 or 6 twisted arms; several finishes. 31″ wide, min. length 23″, normal length 40″, 4″ shade fitters. Adaptation of a privately owned document in Portland, Ore. No. COG.

✪ MACLEAY PARK. Classical Revival castings and gas cocks extending from an elongated, reeded oval center; 2, 3, 4, 5 or 6 arms; several finishes. 28″ wide, min. length 23″, standard length 45″, 4″ shade fitters. Adaptation of a privately owned document in Portland, Ore. No. CCG.

✪ SOUTH SHORE. Classical Revival with 13 arms in 2 tiers; several finishes. 41″ wide, min. length 37″, standard length 60″, 4″ shade fitters. Adaptation of a privately owned document in Portland, Ore. No. C2C13G.

THE RENOVATOR'S SUPPLY

✪ GASELIERS. 2 in solid brass. Turn-of-the-century look. Not based on specific documents.

ROY ELECTRIC COMPANY

✪ GASELIER. Colonial Revival turned-brass center with 2, 3, 4, 6 or 8 arms. 30″ wide, min. length 20″, 4″ shade fitters (2, 3, 4 or 6 arms); 33″ wide, min. length 25″, 4″

right
SILVER PALACE.
Nowell's.

below
VAN NESS. Nowell's.

GASELIER. No. GS4-3.
Roy Electric Company.

shade fitters (4, 6 or 8 arms). No. GS2 (small); No. GS1 (large).

⊛ GASELIER. Colonial Revival turned-brass center with 2, 3 or 4 arms. 31″ wide, min. length 27″, 4″ shade fitters. No. GS4.

⊛ GASELIER. Classical Revival turned-brass center with 2, 3, 4 or 6 arms embellished with Art Nouveau castings. 31″ wide, min. length 30″, 4″ shade fitters. No. GS5.

⊛ GASELIER. Colonial Revival turned-brass center with 2, 3, 4 or 6 arms embellished with Art Nouveau floral castings. 29″ wide, min. length 20″, 4″ shade fitters. No. GS6.

✪ GASELIER. Classical Revival turned-brass center with 2, 3, 4 or 6 arms. 28″ wide, min. length 20″, 4″ shade fitters. No. GS7.

✪ GASELIER. Classical Revival turned-brass center with 2, 3, 4 or 6 arms embellished with Art Nouveau floral castings. 31″ wide, min. length 32″, 4″ shade fitters. No. GS8.

✪ GASELIER. Classical Revival turned-brass center with 2 scrolled arms. 40″ wide, min. length 24″, 4″ shade fitters. No. GS9.

✪ GASELIER. Fluted-urn brass center with 2, 3, 4 or 6 arms. 28″ wide, min. length 24″, 4″ shade fitters. No. GS10.

✪ GASELIER. Simple T-shaped fixture with 2, 3 or 4 arms embellished with large Rococo Revival castings. 32″ wide, min. length 24″, 4″ shade fitters. No. GS11.

✪ GASELIER. 2 Classical Revival urns joined by 3 rods to create a center shaft with 2, 3, 4 or 6 arms embellished with Art Nouveau floral castings. 32″ wide, min. length 36″, 4″ shade fitters. No. GS12.

✪ GASELIER. Large and eclectic with 9 arms embellished with Art Nouveau floral castings in 2 tiers. 46″ wide, min. length 48″, 4″ shade fitters. No. GS13.

GASELIER. No. GS11-2. Roy Electric Company.

ST. LOUIS ANTIQUE LIGHTING COMPANY

✪ GASELIERS. Numerous fixtures in brass. Turn-of-the-century look. Not based on specific documents.

VICTORIAN LIGHTCRAFTERS

✪ GAS-STYLE CHANDELIER. Colonial Revival stem with 2, 3, 4, 5 or 6 scrolled arms terminating in Art Nouveau castings; solid brass; several finishes. 32″ wide, min. length 21″, max. length 59″, 4″ shade fitters. No. C-205.

✪ GAS-STYLE CHANDELIER. Colonial Revival stem with 2, 3 or 4 curved arms terminating in Classical Revival castings; solid brass; several finishes. 22″ wide, min. length 21″, max. length 58″, 4″ shade fitters. No. C-300.

✪ GAS-STYLE CHANDELIER. Eclectic with Colonial Revival stem and 2, 3, 4, 5 or 6 scrolled arms terminating in Art Nouveau castings; solid brass; several finishes. 30″ wide, min. length 22″, max. length 57″, 4″ shade fitters. Adaptation. No. C-450.

✪ GAS-STYLE CHANDELIER. Eclectic with Colonial Revival stem and 2, 3, 4, 5 or 6 scrolled arms terminating in dragon-head castings; solid brass; several finishes.

below left
GAS-STYLE CHANDELIER. No. C-500. Victorian Lightcrafters.

below right
GAS-STYLE CHANDELIER. No. C-900. Victorian Lightcrafters.

30" wide, min. length 24", max. length 57", 4" shade fitters. Adaptation. No. C-500.

⚙ GAS-STYLE CHANDELIER. Colonial Revival with 8 arms in 2 tiers; solid brass; several finishes. 32" wide, min. length 29", max. length 67", 4" shade fitters. Adaptation. No. C-890.

⚙ GAS-STYLE CHANDELIER. 2, 3 or 4 arms; solid brass; several finishes. 28" wide, min. length 30", max. length 58", 4" shade fitters. Adaptation. No. C-900.

⚙ GAS-STYLE CHANDELIER. 2, 3, 4, 5 or 6 arms; solid brass; several finishes. 30" wide, min. length 22", max. length 58", 4" shade fitters. Adaptation. No. C-980.

⚙ GAS-STYLE CHANDELIER. Colonial Revival with 6 arms; solid brass; several finishes. 41" wide, min. length 36", max. length 55", 4" shade fitters. Adaptation. No. C-1000.

VICTORIAN LIGHTING WORKS

⚙ GASELIERS. Brass with 2, 3, 4, 5 or 6 arms. Turn-of-the-century look. Not based on specific documents.

VICTORIAN REPRODUCTION LIGHTING COMPANY

⚙ GASELIERS. 2 in brass. Turn-of-the-century look. Not based on specific documents.

HALL LIGHTS, PENDANTS AND LANTERNS: TURN OF THE CENTURY

BRASSLIGHT

⚙ BELLE HARP. Brass hall light with 1 burner. Late 19th century. 12" wide, 27" high, 4" shade fitter. Adaptation.

D'LIGHTS

⚙ PENDANT. Brass hall light with 1 burner. Late 19th century. 24" high, 4" shade fitter. Adaptation. No. 509-1.

NOWELL'S

⚙ NATOMA. 1 burner with smoke bell; antique or polished brass finish. c. 1880. 9" wide, min. length 24", max. length 42", 4" shade fitter. Adaptation of a document at the Parrot House, Saint Helena, Calif.

⚙ RINCON HILL. 2 Colonial Revival burners with intertwining arms; antique or polished brass finish. Turn of

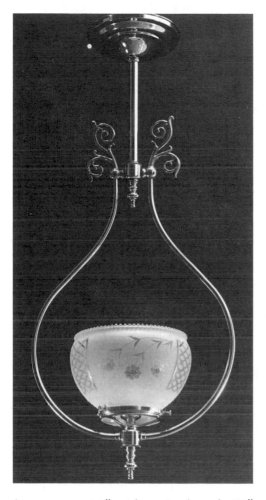

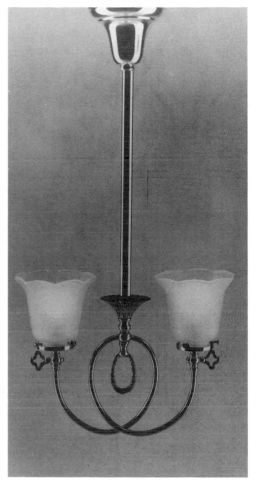

the century. 14″ wide, min. length 17″, max. length 42″, 2¼″ shade fitters. Adaptation.

PROGRESS LIGHTING

✿ ART NOUVEAU. Flowering dogwood design hall light with 1 burner. c. 1900. 7½″ wide, min. length 19″, max. length 28″, 4″ shade fitter. Adaptation of Progress Lighting gaselier no. P-4041. No. P-3606.

THE RENOVATOR'S SUPPLY

✿ HALL FIXTURES. 2 in solid brass. 4″ shade fitters. Turn-of-the-century look. Not based on specific documents.

above left
BELLE HARP.
Brasslight.

above right
RINCON HILL.
Nowell's.

Roy Electric Company

❀ HALL LIGHT. Classical Revival brass center with 2 arms projecting from the mouths of griffins. 28″ wide, min. length 18″, 4″ shade fitters. No. H2-G2.

❀ HALL LIGHT. 1 burner supported by a brass harp. 14″ wide, min. length 18″, 4″ shade fitter. No. H4-G1.

St. Louis Antique Lighting Company

❀ CEILING LIGHTS. 2 in brass. Turn-of-the-century look. Not based on specific documents.

Victorian Lightcrafters

❀ GAS-STYLE CEILING FIXTURE. 1 burner set in a Classical Revival harp; solid brass; several finishes. 11″ wide, min. length 18″, max. length 49″, 4″ shade fitter. No. C-350.

Victorian Reproduction Lighting Company

❀ HALL FIXTURES. 2 T-shaped fixtures with 2 burners and 1 hanging hall lamp in brass. Turn-of-the-century look. Not based on specific documents.

NEWEL-POST FIXTURES: TURN OF THE CENTURY

Nowell's

❀ WELLS FARGO. 1 burner atop an elegant neoclassical post; antique or polished brass finish. Turn of the century. 8″ wide, 24″ high, 4″ shade fitter. Adaptation. Suitable for a Colonial Revival or Classical Revival interior.

WALL BRACKETS: MID- TO LATE 19TH CENTURY

Classic Illumination

❀ GRIFFIN. Griffin holding aloft 1 burner; solid brass; antique or polished finish. c. 1870–80. 7½″ wide, 17″ high, extends 14″, 4″ shade fitter; uses the same arm casting as Classic Illumination gaselier no. 1870. Reproduction of a privately owned document. No. 1875-1.

Nowell's

❀ FLORA. Classical goddess of flowers holding aloft a cornucopia from which 1 burner emerges; antique or polished finish. c. 1860. 22″ high, extends 14″, 4″ shade fitter. Reproduction of a privately owned document in San Francisco. [See page 98.]

PROGRESS LIGHTING

❁ CLASSICAL. Classical crystal prisms with 1 arm. 1840s. 7″ wide, 12½″ high, extends 13″, 2½″ shade fitter. Adaptation of Progress Lighting gas chandelier no. P-4048. No. P-2933.

❁ ROCOCO. Rococo Revival with 1 arm. 1850s. 7″ wide, 10″ high, extends 12″, 2½″ shade fitter. Adaptation of Progress Lighting gas chandelier no. P-4063. No. P-2953.

D'LIGHTS

❁ WALL BRACKETS. 4 brass fixtures with 1 or 2 burners. Turn-of-the-century look. Not based on specific documents.

M-H LAMP AND FAN COMPANY

❁ GAS-STYLE WALL FIXTURES. 3 in brass. Turn-of-the-century look. Not based on specific documents.

above left
GRIFFIN. Classic Illumination.

above right
WELLS FARGO. Nowell's.

WALL BRACKETS: TURN OF THE CENTURY

FLOOD MANSION.
Nowell's.

NOWELL'S

⚙ ASSAY OFFICE. 1 arm; antique or polished brass finish. 8″ high, extends 9½″, 4″ shade fitter. Adaptation. Suitable for a Colonial Revival or Classical Revival interior.

⚙ COMSTOCK. 2 arms; antique or polished brass finish. 21″ wide, 15″ high, extends 11″, 4″ shade fitters.

⚙ FLOOD MANSION. Colonial Revival with porcelain "candles"; 3 burners and flame bulbs without glass shades; antique or polished brass finish. 15½″ wide, 13½″ high without bulbs, extends 11¼″. Common form of turn-of-the-century, rarely reproduced.

⚙ WOODWARD GARDENS. 1 burner; antique or polished brass finish. 13½″ high, extends 13″, 4″ shade fitter.

⚙ YERBA BUENA. Classical Revival with 1 arm and hanging glass prisms; antique or polished brass finish. 11″ high, extends 12″, 4″ shade fitter. Adaptation.

PROGRESS LIGHTING

⚙ ART NOUVEAU. Flowering dogwood design with 1 arm. c. 1900. 7½″ wide, 9″ high, extends 15″, 4″ shade fitter. Adaptation of Progress Lighting gaselier no. P-4041. No. P-2904.

REJUVENATION LAMP AND FIXTURE COMPANY

✪ NEWBERG. 1 arm; several finishes. 8″ wide, 11″ high, extends 16″, 4″ shade fitter. No. WC1G.

THE RENOVATOR'S SUPPLY

✪ LADY HALBURTON. 1 arm with "Diamond Daisy" shade. 7½″ wide, extends 12″, 4″ shade fitter. Late 19th-century look. Not based on a specific document. No. 30519.

✪ LINDHURST. 1 adjustable arm with ruffled glass shade. 5½″ back plate, extends up to 25½″, 4″ shade fitter. Late 19th-century look. Not based on a specific document. Suitable for bathrooms and bedrooms. No. 23198.

GAS WALL BRACKET. No. AS-1. Roy Electric Company.

ROY ELECTRIC COMPANY

✪ GAS WALL BRACKET. 1 or 2 cast arms forming winged figures extending from an oval back plate. 1880s. 7″ wide, 13″ high, extends 10″, 4″ shade fitter (1 arm); 14″ wide, 16″ high, extends 8″, 4″ shade fitter (2 arms). No. AS-1 (1 arm); No. AS-2 (2 arms).

✪ GAS WALL BRACKET. 1 tight-looped arm with griffin casting. 7″ wide, 10½″ high, extends 12″, 2¼″ shade fitter. No. GPS-1.

✪ GAS WALL BRACKET. 1 scrolled arm springing from the mouth of a griffin. 1880s on. 7″ wide, 10″ high, extends 15″, 4″ shade fitter. Adaptation of an unusual fixture. No. GS-1.

✪ GAS WALL BRACKET. 1 arm on a rod extending from a classical back plate. 7″ wide, 12″ high, extends 14″, 4″ shade fitter. No. S2-G-1.

✪ GAS WALL BRACKET. 1 curved arm with a late classical casting as transition from back plate to gas pipe. c. 1900. 7″ wide, 12″ high, extends 14″, 4″ shade fitter. No. S3-G-1.

✪ GAS WALL BRACKET. 1 curved arm joined to a classical back plate. 7″ wide, 12″ high, extends 13″, 4″ shade fitter. No. S-G1.

✪ GAS WALL BRACKET. 1 arm with Art Nouveau cast-

GAS WALL BRACKET. No. GS-1. Roy Electric Company.

ing attached to a Classical Revival oval back plate. 4″ wide, 9″ high, extends 6″, 2¼″ shade fitter. No. SG2-1.

☼ GAS WALL BRACKET. 1 S-curve arm terminating in griffin-head casting. 7″ wide, 14″ high, extends 11″, 4″ shade fitter. No. WS-1.

☼ GAS WALL BRACKET. 1 arm terminating in griffin-head casting embellished with a stylized floral motif. Late 1870s–80s. 7″ wide, 13″ high, extends 15″, 4″ shade fitter. No. WSF-1.

ST. LOUIS ANTIQUE LIGHTING COMPANY

☼ WALL SCONCES. 5 in brass. Turn-of-the-century look. Not based on specific documents.

VICTORIAN LIGHTCRAFTERS

☼ GAS-STYLE WALL FIXTURE. 1 Classical Revival arm terminating in classical scroll castings; solid brass; several finishes. 7″ wide, 11″ high, extends 14″, 4″ shade fitter. No. W-205.

☼ GAS-STYLE WALL FIXTURE. 1 scrolled arm terminating in Classical Revival casting mounted on a Classical Revival back plate; solid brass; several finishes. 7″ wide, 11″ high, extends 11″, 4″ shade fitter. No. W-300.

☼ GAS-STYLE WALL FIXTURE. 2 curved arms terminating in Art Nouveau castings attached to a Colonial Revival ball with turned finials; solid brass; several finishes. 21″ wide, 12″ high, extends 11″, 4″ shade fitter. No. W-310-D.

☼ GAS-STYLE WALL FIXTURE. 1 curved arm terminating in Art Nouveau casting; solid brass; several finishes. 7″ wide, 12″ high, extends 13″, 4″ shade fitter. No. W-450.

☼ GAS-STYLE WALL FIXTURE. 1 S-scroll arm terminating in a cast dragon head; solid brass; several finishes. 7″ wide, 13″ high, extends 14″, 4″ shade fitter. No. W-500.

☼ GAS-STYLE WALL FIXTURE. 1 arm mounted on a reeded rod with a turned Colonial Revival finial below; solid brass; several finishes. 7″ wide, 12″ high, extends 9″, 4″ shade fitter. No. W-610.

☼ GAS-STYLE WALL FIXTURE. 1 S-scroll arm terminating in Art Nouveau casting; solid brass; several finishes. 7″ wide, 9″ high, extends 14″, 4″ shade fitter. No. W-651.

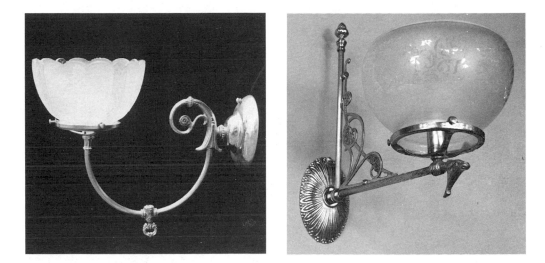

✪ GAS-STYLE WALL FIXTURE. 1 arm gracefully scrolled from a Classical Revival back plate; solid brass; several finishes. 8½″ wide, 13½″ high, extends 13″, 4″ shade fitter. No. W-890.

VICTORIAN LIGHTING WORKS

✪ WALL BRACKETS. 2 in brass with 1 or 2 arms. Turn-of-the-century look. Not based on specific documents.

VICTORIAN REPRODUCTION LIGHTING COMPANY

✪ WALL BRACKETS. 4 in brass with 1 or 2 arms. Turn-of-the-century look. Not based on specific documents.

top left and right
GAS WALL BRACKETS. No. S3-G-1 and No. WSF-1. Roy Electric Company.

above left and right
GAS-STYLE WALL FIXTURES. No. W-310-D and No. W-610. Victorian Lightcrafters.

ELECTRIC LIGHTING:
1879 TO 1930

In retrospect, the advances in artificial lighting between Argand's burner and the opening of Edison's first electrical station in New York City a century later can be dismissed as merely prologue to the inevitable triumph of modern technology. In the late 19th century, however, gas lighting was a marvel so highly refined and economically entrenched that few in the Western world could imagine its being swept aside.

That electrical energy could be made to produce light was well known to science. Humphrey Davy had discovered the "electric arc" light by 1808, but voltaic batteries were unequal to the power requirements of the system. Even after the invention of the generator, arc lighting—created by passing a current between two carbon rods—found favor only for the illumination of streets and large commercial spaces because the resulting light was too intense. Nonetheless, several inventors in the 1860s and 1870s attempted to find a way to harness electricity for residential use by bringing a filament to incandescence within a glass vacuum tube so that the filament would not be consumed.

Enter Thomas A. Edison (1847–1931), already the acclaimed inventor of the multiplex telegraph. Edison sought to develop an inexpensive incandescent bulb and a mass distribution system to compete directly with the gas lighting industry. According to Edison, "I have an idea that I can make the electric light available for all common uses, and supply it at a trifling cost, compared with that of gas. There is no difficulty about dividing up the electric currents and using small quantities at different points. The trouble is in finding a candle that will give a pleasant

Mrs. Cornelius Vanderbilt in her blue velvet and satin "Electric Light" ball gown designed by Frederick Worth, 1883. According to one newspaper account, "hidden in [the] bodice was a convenient little battery which did not interfere with dancing in the least." (New-York Historical Society)

light, not too intense, which can be turned on or off as easily as gas."

Much has been written about Edison's early efforts to solve this problem. Yet his genius lay in synthesizing the discoveries of others and coming up with an economical, practical, integrated system—a system in which the carbon-filament bulb was only the most dramatic part. He designed the dynamos, meters, underground cable system, wiring and switches as well as the deceptively simple bulb itself. Edison moved incandescent lighting out of the laboratory and into homes, offices and factories—a technological leap of far-reaching social and economic consequence. The Edison Electric Light Company came into existence in 1878, and on September 4, 1882, the first system went into operation in New York City. Twenty years later 3,600 American power plants were in operation.

THE LIGHT BULB. Consider for a moment the common electric light bulb, the popular term for what the lighting industry calls a lamp. If it fails to respond to the flick of a switch, we turn with momentary annoyance to a closet or kitchen drawer for a replacement. With a quick glance to check the wattage, our hand grasps the familiar shape and, perhaps with an absentminded shake—hoping not to hear the fatal rattle of broken filament against frosted interior—we twist it into the socket and go about our business. Aside from the assumption that the bulb will more often than not respond, we don't give this technological marvel of standardization much thought.

Edison's first commercially successful lamp of 1879 utilized a hairpin-loop carbon filament enclosed in a free-blown, clear glass bulb. (Early bulbs had a distinctive glass tip that remained after the air was pumped out of the bulb and the hole sealed; tipless bulbs generally date after about 1920, when a glass exhaust tube was incorporated into the center stem.) Although the clear glass bulb allowed the filament to show, the intensity of early lamps was so low that glare was not a problem. This explains in part why some early electrical installations intended for unshielded lamps appear so harsh to modern eyes when fitted with more brilliant modern bulbs. It is not uncommon for late 19th- or early 20th-century commercial and residential structures to have ceiling fixtures and entrance-hall archways wired for exposed lamps.

Throughout the 1880s and 1890s the intensity of carbon-filament bulbs increased as multiple-loop and curled filaments were introduced. Gradually, however, the efficiency of the bulbs—especially after the tungsten filament (1907–11) was perfected—reached the point where the light had to be diffused either by painting or etching the exterior of the glass bulb itself or by designing fixtures that hid the light source with fabric shades and glass bowls. The now ubiquitous bulb with a frosted interior did not become available until about 1925. (For manufacturers of reproduction light bulbs, see pp. 162–63.)

ELECTRIC FIXTURES. As electricity gradually became available in the 1880s and 1890s, lighting fixture manufacturers sensed that it was only a matter of time before the new energy source replaced the old. However, early electricity was an uncertain light source; until the perfection of the tungsten-filament bulb, it was prudent to have both gas and electric fixtures. In response to this need, manufacturers supplied combination fixtures that utilized both

Early 20th-century combination gas-electric fixtures from the Mitchell Vance Company catalog, New York City. (The Athenaeum of Philadelphia)

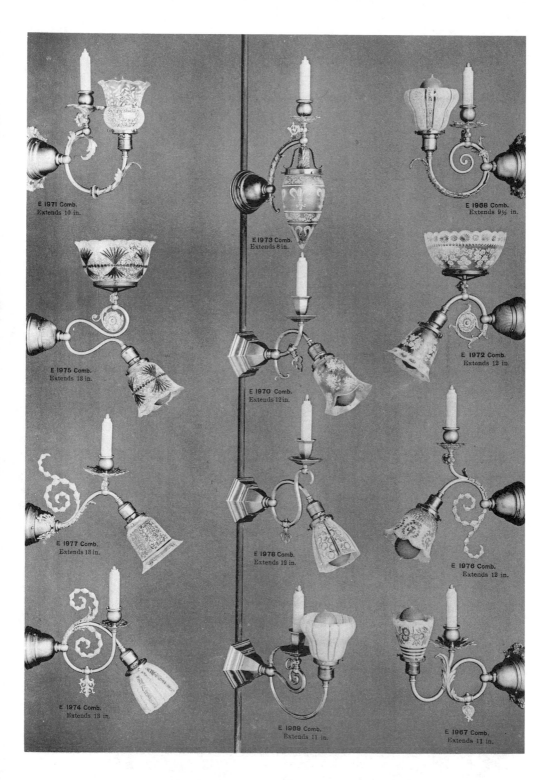

E 1971 Comb.
Extends 10 in.

E 1973 Comb.
Extends 8 in.

E 1968 Comb.
Extends 9½ in.

E 1975 Comb.
Extends 13 in.

E 1972 Comb.
Extends 12 in.

E 1970 Comb.
Extends 12 in.

E 1977 Comb.
Extends 18 in.

E 1978 Comb.
Extends 12 in.

E 1976 Comb.
Extends 12 in.

E 1974 Comb.
Extends 13 in.

E 1969 Comb.
Extends 11 in.

E 1967 Comb.
Extends 11 in.

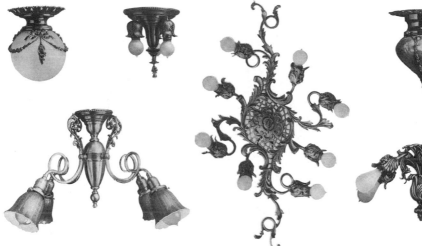

energy sources. Because thousands of buildings erected between the 1880s and World War I are today being restored, there is a brisk demand for reproduction combination fixtures such as gaselier-electroliers and gas-electric hall lights. Most buildings dating to the post-1910 period, however, should be restored with fixtures intended exclusively for electricity unless on-site studies indicate that electricity was not yet available there.

While the first combination fixtures differed little in style from those manufactured for gas, many early electrical installations were purely utilitarian: a bare bulb inserted into a porcelain socket or hung from the ceiling by a wire. Inexpensive as such installations are to recreate, most owners will be distressed by this blatant celebration of technology and may wish to adopt one of the more decorative alternatives, such as pan lights that mount flush to the ceiling, although the bulbs will still be exposed. For commercial installations manufacturers offered corrugated-metal pan reflectors and holophane shades; both were designed to increase the light from carbon-filament bulbs and gradually passed out of favor after tungsten-filament lamps became available. (Several of the manufacturers here offer holophane shades. See also p. 165.)

A NEW AESTHETIC. Flexible electric lighting also encouraged its own aesthetic. Freed from the design constraints of open-flame lighting and requiring only a thin,

Early 20th-century electric ceiling fixtures from the McKenney and Waterbury catalog, Boston. For an authentic appearance, such fixtures require carbon-filament bulbs. (The Athenaeum of Philadelphia)

opposite
Early 20th-century combination gas-electric wall brackets from the Mitchell Vance Company catalog, New York City. (The Athenaeum of Philadelphia)

Art Nouveau electric lighting fixtures discussed in *Decorative Electricity* by Mrs. J. E. H. Gordon, who described bronze stork and crane lights as "very convenient" for drawing rooms but noted that a fringe on a dining table light "however handsome, is not satisfactory." (The Athenaeum of Philadelphia)

Combination gas-electric fixtures from the Pettingell-Andrews catalog, 1904, Boston. Three items are labeled: "L'Art Nouveau" (top right), "Classic" (center) and "Colonial" (bottom right). (The Athenaeum of Philadelphia)

pliable wire to reach the lamp, fixtures could be made in virtually any shape or material that caught the designer's fancy. Advances in electric lighting at the turn of the century happily coincided with the "New Art" movement that, in the words of one historian, resulted in "the single most creative period in the annals of domestic lighting." The Favrile shades of Louis Comfort Tiffany (1848–1933) immediately come to mind; such opalescent glass, made with a technique Tiffany patented in 1880, required not only the intensity of electric light but also the freedom and flexibility of electric wiring. (For manufacturers of Tiffany-style glass shades, see p. 167.) The table lamps, wall brackets and electroliers of Tiffany and the other followers of the new aesthetic dipped deeply into the inspiration of botany, the human (especially female) form and that bizarre hybrid of the two known as *femme-fleur*. One critic complained in 1902 of a table lamp consisting of "a poor little female body in the middle of roses which are, in fact, actually electric lamps, so that the unfortunate girl appears to be on the point of being devoured by the flames."

American Art Nouveau was relatively tame compared to the pure European strain, yet in the popular market floral motifs and art glass became part of the stock-in-trade of American lighting fixture manufacturers throughout the first decades of this century, and many of these are being reproduced today. In degraded form, "New Art" fixtures coexisted with the revived "antique" or traditional styles that owed more to the fertile imaginations of early 20th-century designers than to the European courts of the 18th century from which they claimed inspiration. *House Beautiful* warned in 1897 that modern manufacturers combined "all the decorative motives which the original designers would have spread over half a dozen different objects, and the result is most appalling in its ugliness." Among the reproductions now available, the term "Tiffany shade" has become a generic name for any leaded-glass shade with colored glass, but like early 20th-century mass-produced examples, many of the modern shades bear an only superficial resemblance to the work of the Tiffany Studios.

The same push and pull of competing styles that characterized late 19th- and early 20th-century design is, of course, to be found in the reproduction lighting market. Here, too, we see reflected the emergence of two parallel and complementary streams of "reform" philosophy that would ultimately come to dominate mid-20th-century American design. Both trace their roots to the 1876 Centennial Exhibition held in Philadelphia: the Arts and Crafts movement, reflected in America in the Craftsman interior, and the Colonial Revival. Ten million Americans visited the Philadelphia fair, where they encountered the New England log-house kitchen furnished with spinning wheel, cradle and candlesticks—all icons of the Colonial Revival. Concurrently, visitors came face-to-face with the reform theories espoused by British designers, architects and critics who argued against the ornate, highly decorated objects associated with the "antique" revivals of 18th-century Europe. Popularized by the writings of Charles Eastlake, this reform aesthetic called for a nostalgic return to simplicity and honesty in design, a cry eventually taken up in America by Elbert G. Hubbard (1856–1915) and Gustav Stickley (1857–1942). Wrote one critic looking back on the fair: "A change is coming over the spirit of our time, which has its origin partly . . . in the memorial epoch through which we are passing, but which is also a proof that our taste is getting a root in a healthier and more native soil. All this resuscitation of 'old furniture' and revival of old simplicity . . . is in reality much more sensible than it seems to be to those who look upon it as only another phase of the 'centennial mania.'"

REPRODUCTIONS. The prospective purchaser of lighting fixtures should select reproductions suitable to the style of the structure as well as its technological period. This is especially true when selecting from the many gas-electric combination and electric fixtures. At no previous time in our history was there such a menu of choice, and modern manufacturers of lighting for historic buildings reflect that variety in their offerings. A Craftsman bungalow in Denver, an industrialist's Renaissance mansion in Minneapolis and a Colonial Revival house near Boston might have been erected in the same year and wired for electricity. Differences in geographical location and economic standing aside, it is highly unlikely that the original builders would have selected the same style of lighting fixture, and these differences should be taken into account when selecting reproductions. Visits to houses of the same age and style in your area and the close examination of photographs at the local historical society will provide additional guidance. Books of photographs such as William Seale's *The Tasteful Interlude: American Interiors Through the Camera's Eye, 1860–1917* (Nashville: American Association for State and Local History, 1981) are always useful for such details. Most of the reproductions that follow are suitable generally for the turn-of-the-century period, 1880–1920.

CLASSIC ILLUMINATION

⊛ CHANDELIER. 4, 6 or 8 arms (half gas, half electric); solid brass; several finishes. 1890. 27" wide, various lengths, 4" and 2¼" shade fitters.

D'LIGHTS

⊛ CHANDELIERS. 8 Colonial Revival fixtures. Late 19th to early 20th century. Adaptations.

GASELIER-
ELECTROLIERS

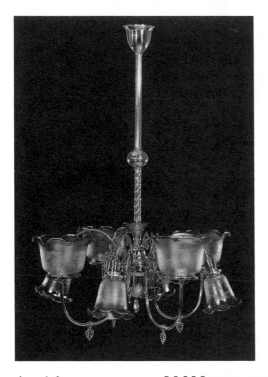 

above left
CHANDELIER. Classic
Illumination.

above right
LOUISE BOYD.
Nowell's.

M-H LAMP AND FAN COMPANY

✪ GAS-ELECTRIC CHANDELIERS. 2 in brass with 2, 4, 5 or 6 arms. Turn-of-the-century look. Not based on specific documents.

NOWELL'S

✪ COAST EXCHANGE. Neoclassical urn center with 4 arms (half gas, half electric); antique or polished brass finish. 27″ wide, min. length 24″, max. length 42″, 4″ and 2¼″ shade fitters.

✪ DIAMOND HEIGHTS. Neoclassical urn center with 6 arms (half gas, half electric); antique or polished brass finish. 24″ wide, min. length 24″, max. length 40″, 4″ and 2¼″ shade fitters.

✪ EMPEROR NORTON. Neoclassical center with 12 arms (half gas, half electric) in 2 tiers; antique or polished brass finish. 50″ wide, min. length 36″, max. length 72″, 4″ and 2¼″ shade fitters. Adaptation of a document at the Parrot House, Saint Helena, Calif. Suitable for a public space.

✪ LOUISE BOYD. Neoclassical center with 6 arms (half

gas, half electric); antique or polished brass finish. 28″ wide, min. length 24″, max. length 42″, 4″ and 2¼″ shade fitters. Adaptation of a document at the Louise Boyd House, San Rafael, Calif.

⊛ MERCHANT STREET. Neoclassical reeded urn center with 4 arms (half gas, half electric); antique or polished brass finish. 28″ wide, min. length 24″, max. length 42″, 4″ and 2¼″ shade fitters.

⊛ MONADNOCK. Neoclassical reeded urn center with 6 arms (half gas, half electric); antique or polished brass finish. 28″ wide, min. length 24″, max. length 42″, 4″ and 2¼″ shade fitters.

⊛ PACIFIC CLUB. Neoclassical center of reeded urns and turnings with 6 arms (half gas, half electric); antique or polished brass finish. 36″ wide, min. length 36″, max. length 42″, 4″ and 2¼″ shade fitters. Adaptation of a privately owned document in San Francisco.

⊗ TESSIE WALL. Neoclassical urn center with 8 arms (half gas, half electric); antique or polished brass finish. 28" wide, min. length 24", max. length 42", 4" and 2¼" shade fitters.

PROGRESS LIGHTING

⊗ COLONIAL. 6 gracefully scrolled arms (half gas, half electric) arranged around a Colonial Revival center of reeded balls with large neoclassical gas cocks; opalescent, pleated shades. c. 1900. 34" wide, min. length 23", max. length 49", 4" shade fitters. Reproduction from a catalog of the Gibson Fixture Works, Philadelphia, at The Athenaeum of Philadelphia. No. P-4067.

REJUVENATION LAMP AND FIXTURE COMPANY

below left
COLONIAL. Progress Lighting.

below right
COUNCIL CREST. Rejuvenation Lamp and Fixture Company.

⊗ COUNCIL CREST. Simple, Colonial Revival T-shaped fixture with 4, 6 or 8 lights (half gas, half electric) on 2, 3 or 4 arms; several finishes. 25" wide, min. length 19", standard length 40", 4" and 2¼" shade fitters. Adaptation of a privately owned document in Portland, Ore. No. CVG/E.

⊗ FOREST PARK. Classical detailing on a ribbed center and 4, 6 or 8 arms; several finishes. 28" wide, standard

length 23″, max. length 45″, 4″ and 2¼″ shade fitters. Adaptation of a privately owned document in Portland, Ore. No. CCE/G.

⊛ PIEDMONT. 4, 6 or 8 simple brass arms curving from a banded ball; several finishes. 28″ wide, min. length 18″, standard length 45″, 4″ and 2¼″ shade fitters. Adaptation of a privately owned document in Portland, Ore. No. CBE/G.

ROY ELECTRIC COMPANY

⊛ GAS-ELECTRIC CHANDELIER. Colonial Revival stem with 4 or 6 curved arms (half gas, half electric) terminating in Art Nouveau castings. 30″ wide, min. length 20″, 4″ and 2¼″ shade fitters. No. GES1.

⊛ GAS-ELECTRIC CHANDELIER. Colonial Revival stem of graduated brass balls with 4 or 6 arms (half gas, half electric) and large Classical Revival castings. 28″ wide, min. length 23″, 4″ and 2¼″ shade fitters. No. GES2.

⊛ GAS-ELECTRIC CHANDELIER. Colonial Revival stem with 4 or 6 curved arms (half gas, half electric). 30″ wide, min. length 24″, 4″ and 2¼″ shade fitters. No. GES3.

⊛ GAS-ELECTRIC CHANDELIER. Large Colonial Revival ball stem with 4, 6 or 8 curved arms (half gas, half electric) and Art Nouveau castings. 33″ wide, min. length 36″, 4″ and 2¼″ shade fitters. No. GES5.

⊛ GAS-ELECTRIC CHANDELIER. Colonial Revival ball stem with 4 or 6 curved arms (half gas, half electric). 31″ wide, min. length 30″, 4″ and 2¼″ shade fitters. No. GES6.

⊛ GAS-ELECTRIC CHANDELIER. Colonial Revival ball stem with 4 or 6 curved arms (half gas, half electric) terminating in Art Nouveau castings. 28″ wide, min. length 24″, 4″ and 2¼″ shade fitters. No. GES7.

⊛ GAS-ELECTRIC CHANDELIER. 2 Colonial Revival balls connected by rods with 9 or 12 curving arms (half gas, half electric) in 2 tiers. 36″ or 40″ wide, min. length 40″, 4″ and 2¼″ shade fitters. No. GES8.

ST. LOUIS ANTIQUE LIGHTING COMPANY

⊛ GAS-ELECTRIC CEILING LIGHTS. 3 in brass. Turn-of-the-century look. Not based on specific documents.

VICTORIAN LIGHTCRAFTERS

✪ GAS-ELECTRIC CHANDELIER. 4 or 6 arms; solid brass; several finishes. 31″ wide, min. length 22″, max. length 58″, 4″ and 2¼″ shade fitters. Adaptation. No. C-311.

✪ GAS-ELECTRIC CHANDELIER. 4 or 6 arms; solid brass; several finishes. 31″ wide, min. length 23″, max. length 64″, 4″ and 2¼″ shade fitters. Adaptation. No. C-550.

✪ GAS-ELECTRIC CHANDELIER. 2 or 4 arms (each with 1 gas and 2 electric lights); solid brass; several finishes. 26″ wide, min. length 26″, max. length 63″, 4″ and 2¼″ shade fitters. Adaptation. No. C-625.

VICTORIAN LIGHTING WORKS

✪ GAS-ELECTRIC CHANDELIERS. 3 in brass with 4 or 6 arms. Turn-of-the-century look. Not based on specific documents.

VICTORIAN REPRODUCTION LIGHTING COMPANY

✪ GAS-ELECTRIC CHANDELIERS. 5 in brass. Turn-of-the-century look. Not based on specific documents.

D'LIGHTS

✪ ELECTROLIERS. Numerous fixtures, most Colonial Revival. 20th century. Adaptations.

M-H LAMP AND FAN COMPANY

✪ ELECTROLIERS. 3 in brass with 2, 3, 4, 5, 6 or 8 arms. Turn-of-the-century look. Not based on specific documents.

NOWELL'S

✪ ARBORDALE. Neoclassical urn center with 3 lights; antique or polished brass finish. 22″ wide, min. length 15″, max. length 39″, 2¼″ shade fitters. Adaptation based on a Colorado period photograph.

✪ BARBARY COAST. Pool-table fixture with 4 lights with green glass shades; antique or polished brass finish. 1904. 31″ wide, min. length 24″, max. length 44″, 2¼″ shade fitters. Adaptation from the Pettingell-Andrews catalog.

BARBARY COAST.
Nowell's.

⚙ OLD WALDORF. Neoclassical urn center with 5 lights; antique or polished brass finish. 22" wide, min. length 15", max. length 39", 2¼" shade fitters.

THE RENOVATOR'S SUPPLY

⚙ ELECTROLIERS. 6 in solid brass. Late 19th-century look. Not based on specific documents.

REJUVENATION LAMP AND FIXTURE COMPANY

⚙ MARQUAM HILL. Classical Revival with 2, 3, 4, 5 or 6 lights; several finishes. c. 1900. 25" wide, min. length 17", standard length 44", 2¼" shade fitters. Adaptation of a privately owned document in Portland, Ore. No. CBE.

⚙ MULTNOMAH. Classical Revival with 2, 3, 4, 5, or 6 lights; several finishes. c. 1900. 26" wide, min. length 15", standard length 36", 2¼" shade fitters. Adaptation of a privately owned document in Portland, Ore. No. CRE.

⚙ OVERLOOK. 4 lights suspended from a polished brass body that hangs from the ceiling on 3 chains; several finishes. c. 1905–10. 18" wide, min. length 26", standard length 36", 2¼" shade fitters. Gold plastic lamp cord

above left
OVERLOOK. Rejuvenation Lamp and Fixture Company.

above right
ELECTROLIER. No. EPC1. Roy Electric Company.

for UL listing; cloth lamp cord available by special order. Adaptation closely based on a document in manufacturer's collection. No. CN4E.

⚙ SELLWOOD. Classical Revival with 2, 3, 4, 5 or 6 lights; several finishes. c. 1900. 24″ wide, min. length 23″, standard length 41″, 2¼″ shade fitters. Adaptation of a privately owned document in Portland, Ore. No. COE.

⚙ WESTMORELAND. Center shaft and downward-arcing arms with 3, 4, 5, 6 or 7 lights; several finishes. 28″ wide, min. length 17″, standard length 31″, 2¼″ shade fitters. Adaptation. No. CGE.

ROY ELECTRIC COMPANY

⚙ ELECTROLIER. Colonial Revival ball center with 2, 3, 4 or 6 curved arms. Early 20th century. 30″ wide, min. length 20″, 2¼″ shade fitters. No. EC1.

⚙ ELECTROLIER. Classical Revival center with 3, 4 or 5 arms. Early 20th century. 20″ wide, min. length 20″, 4″ shade fitters. No. EC2.

⚙ ELECTROLIER. "Shower" of 2, 3 or 4 lights suspended by chains from a central urn hung from a chain. c. 1920. 18″ wide, min. length 18″, 2¼″ shade fitters.

 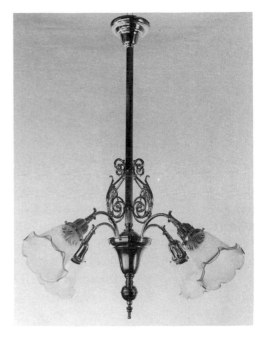

Length of main chain should be adjusted to bring fixture to 6½′ above the floor. No. EPC1.

ST. LOUIS ANTIQUE LIGHTING COMPANY

❂ ELECTROLIERS. 10 in brass. Turn-of-the-century look. Not based on specific documents.

VICTORIAN LIGHTCRAFTERS

❂ ELECTRIC CHANDELIER. Colonial Revival with 2, 3, 4, 5 or 6 floral Art Nouveau arms; solid brass; several finishes. 30″ wide, min. length 18″, max. length 47″, 2¼″ shade fitters. Adaptation. No. C-101.

❂ ELECTRIC CHANDELIER. Classical Revival with 2, 3, 4, 5 or 6 arms; solid brass; several finishes. 28″ wide, min. length 24″, max. length 56″, 2¼″ shade fitters. Adaptation. No. C-201.

❂ ELECTRIC CHANDELIER. Colonial Revival with 2, 3, or 4 arms; solid brass; several finishes. 32″ wide, min. length 18″, max. length 59″, 2¼″ shade fitters. Adaptation. No. C-400.

❂ ELECTRIC CHANDELIER. "Shower" with 4, 5 or 6 arms cascading from a central stem; solid brass; several finishes. Early 20th century. 23″ wide, min. length 28″,

above left
ELECTRIC CHANDE-LIER. No. C-101. Victorian Lightcrafters.

above right
ELECTRIC CHANDE-LIER. No. C-201. Victorian Lightcrafters.

max. length 67″, 2¼″ shade fitters. Adaptation. No. C-420.

✪ ELECTRIC CHANDELIER. Colonial Revival with 2, 3, 4, 5 or 6 arms; solid brass; several finishes. 32″ wide, min. length 20″, max. length 57″, 2¼″ shade fitters. Adaptation. No. C-475.

✪ ELECTRIC CHANDELIER. 2, 3, 4, 5 or 6 arms; solid brass; several finishes. Early 20th century. 28″ wide, min. length 16″, max. length 60″, 2¼″ shade fitters. Adaptation. No. C-605.

✪ ELECTRIC CHANDELIER. Classical Revival with 2, 3, 4, 5 or 6 arms; solid brass; several finishes. 26″ wide, min. length 26″, max. length 63″, 2¼″ and 3¼″ shade fitters. Adaptation. No. C-851.

✪ ELECTRIC CHANDELIER. 2, 3, 4, 5 or 6 arms; opalescent teardrop shade suitable; solid brass; several finishes. Early 20th century. 26″ wide, min. length 24″, max. length 65″, 3¼″ shade fitters. Adaptation. No. C-920.

✪ ELECTRIC CHANDELIER. 2, 3, 4, 5 or 6 arms; solid

below left
ELECTRIC CHANDE-LIER. No. C-851. Victorian Lightcrafters.

below right
WILSHIRE. Rejuvenation Lamp and Fixture Company.

brass; several finishes. Early 20th century. 26″ wide, min. length 19″, max. length 63″, 2¼″ shade fitters. Adaptation. No. C-975.

VICTORIAN LIGHTING WORKS

☻ ELECTRIC CHANDELIERS. 3 in brass with 2, 3, 4, 5 or 6 arms. Turn-of-the-century look. Not based on specific documents.

VICTORIAN REPRODUCTION LIGHTING COMPANY

☻ ELECTROLIERS. 6 in brass with 2, 4 or 6 arms. Turn-of-the-century look. Not based on specific documents.

REJUVENATION LAMP AND FIXTURE COMPANY

☻ BEAUMONT. Mission style in brass with 2 or 4 arms; several finishes. Early 20th century. 23″ wide, 13″ long, 2¼″ shade fitters. Adaptation closely based on an illustration in the R. Williamson and Company catalog. Jo Ann Thomas, ed., *Early Twentieth Century Lighting Fixtures*, p. 95. No. CF2E (2 arms); No. CF4E (4 arms).

☻ WILSHIRE. Mission style in brass with 2 or 4 arms; several finishes. Early 20th century. 22″ wide, min. length 20″, standard length 36″, 2¼″ shade fitters. Reproduction of a document in manufacturer's collection. No. CY2E (2 arms); No. CY4E (4 arms).

RENAISSANCE MARKETING

☻ LILY. Art Nouveau with a cluster of 4–18 floral stems; cast bronze patinated with a Tiffany-style green brown finish; silver lustre art glass shades. Adaptation.

ST. LOUIS ANTIQUE LIGHTING COMPANY

☻ MISSION OAK. Unusual Arts and Crafts wooden frame and chain with glass inserts; several colors. 22″ wide, 36″ high. No. M01.

CLASSIC ILLUMINATION

☻ HALL LIGHT. 2 arms (1 gas, 1 electric); solid brass; several finishes. 17″ wide, various lengths, 4″ and 2¼″ shade fitters. Reproduction of a privately owned document. No. 1890-1.

ELECTROLIERS: ARTS AND CRAFTS STYLE

GAS-ELECTRIC HALL LIGHTS, PENDANTS AND LANTERNS

MACONDRAY LANE.
Nowell's.

M-H Lamp and Fan Company

⚙ GAS-ELECTRIC CEILING PENDANT. Brass. Turn-of-the-century look. Not based on a specific document.

Nowell's

⚙ MACONDRAY LANE. 2 arms (1 gas, 1 electric); antique or polished brass finish. 15″ wide, min. length 18″, max. length 45″, 4″ and 2¼″ shade fitters. Adaptation of a privately owned document in San Francisco. Suitable for halls, stairs and kitchens.

Progress Lighting

⚙ COLONIAL. 2 arms (1 gas, 1 electric). c. 1900. 17″ x 9″ wide, min. length 19″, max. length 27½″, 4″ and 2¼″

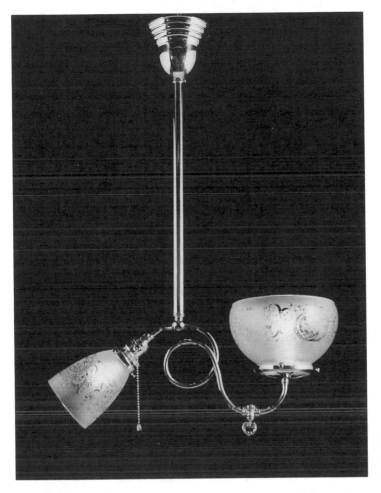

MOCK'S CREST. Rejuvenation Lamp and Fixture Company.

shade fitters. Adaptation of Progress Lighting gas-electric chandelier no. P-4067. No. P-3668.

REJUVENATION LAMP AND FIXTURE COMPANY

✪ MOCK'S CREST. Pendant with 2 lights (1 gas, 1 electric); several finishes. Turn-of-the-century. 18″ wide, min. length 15″, standard length 36″, 4″ and 2¼″ shade fitters. Adaptation closely based on a document in manufacturer's collection. No. CQ1E1G.

ST. LOUIS ANTIQUE LIGHTING COMPANY

✪ GAS-ELECTRIC CEILING PENDANT. Brass. Turn-of-the-century look. Not based on a specific document. No. G1-E1.

ELECTRIC HALL LIGHTS, PENDANTS AND LANTERNS: TURN OF THE CENTURY

VICTORIAN REPRODUCTION LIGHTING COMPANY

✪ HALL LIGHTS. 2 in brass with 3 lights (1 gas, 2 electric). Turn-of-the-century look. Not based on specific documents.

D'LIGHTS

✪ PENDANTS. Numerous fixtures. 1900–30. Adaptations.

M-H LAMP AND FAN COMPANY

✪ ELECTRIC CEILING PENDANT. Brass. Turn-of-the-century look. Not based on a specific document.

NOWELL'S

✪ NATIONAL HOTEL. Neoclassical center with 2 arms; antique or polished brass finish. Early 20th century. 22″ wide, min. length 15″, max. length 39″, 2¼″ shade fitters. Suitable for halls, baths and kitchens.

NATIONAL HOTEL. Nowell's.

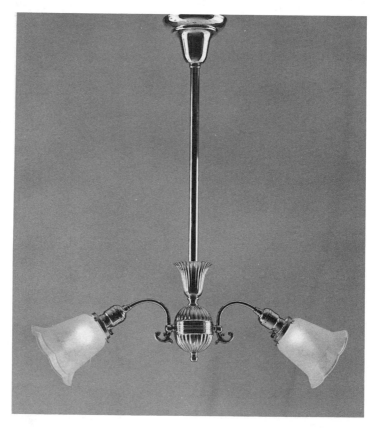

THE RENOVATOR'S SUPPLY

☉ HALL AND BATHROOM FIXTURES. 14 in solid brass. Late 19th- and early 20th-century look. 2¼" and 4" shade fitters. Not based on specific documents.

REJUVENATION LAMP AND FIXTURE COMPANY

☉ HALL LIGHT. 1 light suspended from a chain with a white glass shade. 5" wide, 36" long, 2¼" shade fitter. Adaptation of a document in manufacturer's collection. Gold plastic lamp cord for UL listing; cloth lamp cord available by special order. No. CH2¼.

☉ HALL LIGHT. 1 light suspended from a pipe with an enclosed white glass shade. Early 20th century. 8" wide, 28" long, 4" shade fitter. Adaptation of a document in manufacturer's collection. No. CU4.

VICTORIAN LIGHTCRAFTERS

☉ CEILING FIXTURE. Classical Revival with 1 light suspended from a spiral-turned solid-brass pipe with an enclosed, etched shade; several finishes. Early 20th century. 8" wide, min. length 21", max. length 44", 3¼" shade fitter. No. C-125.

☉ CEILING FIXTURE. 1 light; solid brass; several finishes; mounts close to ceiling. Early 20th century. 8" wide, 9½" long, 2¼" or 3¼" shade fitter. No. C-703.

☉ CEILING FIXTURE. "Shower" with 3 lights suspended from chains; solid brass; several finishes; flush mounted. Early 20th century. 16" wide, min. length 11", max. length 30", 2¼" shade fitter. No. C-950.

VICTORIAN REPRODUCTION LIGHTING COMPANY

☉ HALL LIGHTS. 3 in brass with 1 light. Turn-of-the-century look. Not based on specific documents.

ARROYO CRAFTSMAN

☉ BROWNSTONE. Arts and Crafts lantern in 3 sizes; solid brass; verdigris patina finish. Early 20th century. 12"–20" wide, 13½"–22½" high. Adaptations inspired by fixtures designed by California architects Charles and Henry Greene. Randell L. Makinson, *Greene and Greene: Furniture and Related Designs* (Santa Barbara: Peregrine Smith, 1979).

HALL LIGHT. No. CH2¼. Rejuvenation Lamp and Fixture Company.

ELECTRIC HALL LIGHTS, PENDANTS AND LANTERNS: 20TH CENTURY

above left
MISSION. Arroyo
Craftsman.

above right
MONTEREY. Arroyo
Craftsman.

✪ CRAFTSMAN. Large Arts and Crafts lantern; solid brass; verdigris patina finish; brass-filigree overlay of pine needles and sycamore limbs available. 36″ wide, 17″ high. Adaptation inspired by the designs of Greene and Greene in a particularly useful size.

✪ MISSION. Arts and Crafts lantern in 2 designs and 2 sizes; solid brass; verdigris patina finish. Early 20th century. 5″–7″ wide, 5¾″–11″ high. Adaptation of bungalow fixtures.

✪ MONTEREY. Arts and Crafts lantern in 3 sizes; solid brass; verdigris patina finish; brass-filigree overlay of pine needles and sycamore limbs available. Early 20th century. Adaptation inspired by the designs of Greene and Greene.

B AND P LAMP SUPPLY

✪ PENDANT. 1 light suspended from a chain; enclosed shade. 26″ long. No. 60612.

D'LIGHTS

✪ PENDANTS. Numerous fixtures. Early 20th century. Adaptations.

M-H LAMP AND FAN COMPANY

✪ PENDANTS. 3 in brass. Early 20th-century look. Not based on specific documents.

far left
HALL LIGHT. No.
H3-E1. Roy Electric
Company.

left
SOUTH PARK.
Nowell's.

REJUVENATION LAMP AND FIXTURE COMPANY

⊙ AINSWORTH. 1-pole, Mission-style pendant suspended from a square stem, several finishes. c. 1900. 6" wide, 14" min. length, 30" standard length, 2¼" shade fitter. Adaptation closely based on an illustration in the R. Williamson and Company catalog. Jo Ann Thomas, ed., *Early Twentieth Century Lighting Fixtures*, p. 78. No. CY1E.

ROY ELECTRIC COMPANY

⊙ HALL LIGHT. 1 light suspended from a chain; enclosed shade. 7½" wide, 12" min. length. No. H3-E1.

VICTORIAN REPRODUCTION LIGHTING COMPANY

⊙ HALL FIXTURES. 2 in brass; hung from a chain. Early 20th century look. Not based on specific documents.

NOWELL'S

⊙ SOUTH PARK. 4 lights (1 gas, 3 electric) atop an elegant neoclassical post; antique or polished brass finish. 21" wide, 27" high, 4" and 2½" shade fitters.

VICTORIAN LIGHTCRAFTERS

⊙ GAS-ELECTRIC NEWEL-POST FIXTURE. Solid brass with 4 lights (1 gas, 3 electric); several finishes. 16"

GAS-ELECTRIC NEWEL-POST FIXTURES

wide, min. height 23″, max. height 28″, 2¼″ and 4″ shade fitters. No. N-100.

GAS-ELECTRIC WALL BRACKETS

D'LIGHTS

✪ MULTI-ARM BRACKET. 3 lights (2 gas, 1 electric). Turn of the century. 26″ wide, extends 18″, 4″ and 2¼″ shade fitters. Adaptation.

M-H LAMP AND FAN COMPANY

✪ WALL BRACKETS. 2 in brass with 2 arms (1 gas, 1 electric). Turn-of-the-century look. Not based on specific documents.

NOWELL'S

✪ PORTSMOUTH SQUARE. 2 lights (1 gas, 1 electric); antique or polished brass finish. 12″ high, extends 12″, 4″ and 2¼″ shade fitters. Adaptation.

PROGRESS LIGHTING

✪ COLONIAL. Colonial with 2 arms (1 gas, 1 electric). 12″ wide, 15¾″ high, extends 14½″, 4″ and 2¼″ shade fitters. Adaptation of Progress Lighting gaselier-electrolier no. P-4067. No. P-2954.

REJUVENATION LAMP AND FIXTURE COMPANY

✪ ALBANY. 3 lights (1 gas, 2 electric); several finishes. 23″ wide, 15″ high, extends 13″, 4″ and 2¼″ shade fitters. Adaptation of a privately owned document. No. WC1G2E.

✪ ASTORIA. 2 lights (1 gas, 1 electric); several finishes. Early 20th century. 8″ wide, 13″ high, extends 10″, 4″ and 2¼″ shade fitters. Adaptation of a privately owned document. No. WE1E1G.

THE RENOVATOR'S SUPPLY

✪ VICTORIA'S FAVORITE. 2 arms (1 gas, 1 electric); solid brass; 7½″ wide, 12″ high, extends 12″, 4″ and 2¼″ shade fitters. Turn-of-the-century look. Not based on a specific document. No. 33008.

ROY ELECTRIC COMPANY

✪ GAS-ELECTRIC WALL BRACKET. Simple, 2 lights (1

gas, 1 electric) attached to a rod projecting from a round back plate. 8″ wide, 14″ high, extends 10″, 4″ and 2¼″ shade fitters. No. SGE1.

❂ GAS-ELECTRIC WALL BRACKET. Rococo Revival with 3 lights (2 gas, 1 electric) on curved arms springing from an oval back plate. 20½″ wide, 14″ high, extends 13″, 4″ and 2¼″ shade fitters. No. SGE2.

❂ GAS-ELECTRIC WALL BRACKET. Classical Revival with 3 lights (1 gas, 2 electric) on curved arms attached to a horizonal oval back plate. 12″ wide, 13″ high, extends 10″, 4″ and 2¼″ shade fitters. No. SGE3.

❂ GAS-ELECTRIC WALL BRACKET. Simple, 3 lights (1 gas, 2 electric) on curved arms attached to an oval back plate. 16″ wide, 15″ high, extends 12″, 4″ and 2¼″ shade fitters. No. SGE4.

ST. LOUIS ANTIQUE LIGHTING COMPANY

❂ WALL SCONCES. 2 in brass. Turn-of-the-century look. Not based on specific documents.

VICTORIAN LIGHTCRAFTERS

❂ GAS-ELECTRIC WALL FIXTURE. Simple, 2 lights (1 gas, 1 electric); solid brass; several finishes. 13″ wide, 14″ high, extends 10″, 2¼″ and 4″ shade fitters. Adaptation. No. W-175.

❂ GAS-ELECTRIC WALL FIXTURE. Classical Revival with 3 lights (1 gas, 2 electric); solid brass; several finishes. 17″ wide, 17″ high, extends 10″, 2¼″ and 4″ shade fitters. Adaptation. No. W-290.

❂ GAS-ELECTRIC WALL FIXTURE. Classical Revival with 3 lights (1 gas, 2 electric); solid brass; several finishes. 11″ wide, 17″ high, extends 9″, 2¼″ and 4″ shade fitters. Adaptation. No. W-625.

VICTORIAN REPRODUCTION LIGHTING COMPANY

❂ WALL BRACKETS. 4 in brass with 2 lights (1 gas, 1 electric). Turn-of-the-century look. Not based on specific documents.

D'LIGHTS

❂ MULTI-ARM BRACKETS. Numerous fixtures. Adaptations.

ELECTRIC WALL BRACKETS: TURN OF THE CENTURY

M-H LAMP AND FAN COMPANY

◉ WALL FIXTURES. 7 in brass. Turn-of-the-century look. Not based on specific documents.

NOWELL'S

◉ TILLMAN PLACE. 1 arm; antique or polished brass finish. 9″ high, extends 9″, 2¼″ shade fitter.

REJUVENATION LAMP AND FIXTURE COMPANY

◉ ASHLAND. 1 light; several finishes; brass wall plate for modern electrical box. c. 1900. 5″ wide, 9″ high, extends 15″, 2¼″ shade fitter. Adaptation of a privately owned document. No. WC1E.

◉ DEPOE BAY. 1 light with a fluted oval back plate (will not cover octagonal electrical box); several finishes. 20th century. 5″ wide, 10″ high, extends 8″, 2¼″ shade fitter. No. WA1E.

◉ FOREST GROVE. 1 light; several finishes; brass wall plate for modern electrical box. 20th century. 5″ wide, 11″ high, extends 9″, 2¼″ shade fitter. No. WL1E.

◉ FRENCHGLEN. Colonial Revival with 2 lights and an oval back plate (will not cover octagonal electrical box); several finishes. 20th century. 12″ wide, 6″ high, extends 6″, 2½″ shade fitter. No. W02E-B.

◉ HOOD RIVER. 1 light; several finishes. 5″ wide, 10″ high, extends 8″, 2¼″ shade fitter. Adaptation. No. WM1E.

◉ JEWELL. Colonial Revival with 1 light and an oval back plate (will not cover octagonal electrical box); several finishes. 20th century. 5″ wide, 9″ high, extends 7″, 2¼″ shade fitter. No. W01E.

◉ PENDLETON. 2 lights; several finishes. 18″ wide, 10″ high, extends 9″, 2¼″ shade fitters. Adaptation. No. WD2E.

◉ ST. HELENS. 1 light; several finishes. 7″ wide, 9″ high, extends 10″, 2¼″ shade fitter. Adaptation. No. WD1E.

◉ SUBLIMITY. 1 light; several finishes. 5″ wide, 8″ high, extends 8″, 2¼″ shade fitter. Adaptation. No. WD1E-M.

THE RENOVATOR'S SUPPLY

❂ WALL BRACKETS. 3 in solid brass with 1 or 2 arms. Turn-of-the-century look. Not based on specific documents.

ROY ELECTRIC COMPANY

❂ WALL BRACKET. Cast griffin head and Classical Revival cast back plate with 1 light. Late 19th century. 4½″ wide, 12″ high, extends 13″, 2¼″ shade fitter. No. D-1.
❂ WALL BRACKET. Oval Classical Revival cast back plate with 2 lights. Early 20th century. 16″ wide, 16″ high, extends 13″, 2¼″ shade fitter. No. D-2.
❂ WALL BRACKET. Simple spun back plate with 1 light suspended under a projecting rod. 6″ wide, 11½″ high, extends 9″, 2¼″ shade fitter. No. MS-1.
❂ WALL BRACKET. Simple oval back plate with curved projecting arm with 1 light. 6″ wide, 12″ high, extends 11″, 2¼″ shade fitter. No. S1-E.
❂ WALL BRACKET. Simple oval back plate with curved projecting arm with 1 light. 5″ wide, 11″ high, extends 11″, 2¼″ shade fitter. No. S2-E.
❂ WALL BRACKET. Round back plate with curved arm with 1 light terminating in Art Nouveau casting. 12″ wide, 13″ high, extends 10″, 2¼″ shade fitter. No. S3-E.
❂ WALL BRACKET. Classical Revival cast arms with 2 lights attached to a horizontal, classical oval back plate. 10″ wide, 7″ high, extends 6″, 2¼″ shade fitter. No. S4-E.
❂ WALL BRACKET. Curved arms with late classical casting and 2 lights attached to a classical oval back plate. 13″ wide, 15″ high, extends 9″, 2¼″ shade fitter. No. SED1.
❂ WALL BRACKET. Curved arms with 3 lights terminating in cast scrolls attached to a classical oval back plate. 10″ wide, 12″ high, extends 8″, 2¼″ shade fitter. No. SED3.

ST. LOUIS ANTIQUE LIGHTING COMPANY

❂ WALL SCONCES. 5 in brass. Turn-of-the-century look. Not based on specific documents.

VICTORIAN LIGHTCRAFTERS

⚙ WALL FIXTURE. 1 light springing from a cast, floral arm; solid brass; several finishes. 5" wide, 8" high, extends 13", 2¼" shade fitter. No. W-101.

⚙ WALL FIXTURE. 1 light with a fluted socket cover on a curved arm; solid brass; several finishes. 5" wide, 10" high, extends 9", 2¼" shade fitter. No. W-260.

⚙ WALL FIXTURE. Colonial Revival-Classical Revival with 2 lights and fluted socket covers on curving arms mounted on a cast ball with fluted finials; solid brass; several finishes. 7" wide, 12" high, extends 9", 2¼" shade fitters. Adaptation. No. W-280.

⚙ WALL FIXTURE. 1 light on an S-scroll arm; solid brass; several finishes. 5" wide, 10" high, extends 13", 2¼" shade fitter. W-400.

⚙ WALL FIXTURE. 1 light suspended from a graceful Classical Revival arm; solid brass; several finishes. 5" wide, 13" high, extends 11", 2¼" shade fitter. No. W-420.

⚙ WALL FIXTURE. 1 light with a fluted socket cover on a scrolled arm terminating in a cast, classical scroll; solid brass; several finishes. 5" wide, 12" high, extends 14", 2¼" shade fitter. No. W-475.

⚙ WALL FIXTURE. 1 light with a fluted socket cover on a scrolled arm terminating in a floral casting; solid brass; several finishes. 5" wide, 12" high, extends 12", 2¼" shade fitter. No. W-550.

⚙ WALL FIXTURE. 1 light suspended from a simple rod; solid brass; several finishes. 5" wide, 10" high, extends 7", 2¼" shade fitter. No. W-590.

⚙ WALL FIXTURE. 2 lights suspended from a simple rod; solid brass; several finishes. 17½" wide, 9½" high, extends 8", 2¼" shade fitters. No. W-590-2.

⚙ WALL FIXTURE. 1 light hanging below a reeded Classical Revival rod; solid brass; several finishes. 5" wide, 10" high, extends 8", 2¼" shade fitter. No. W-600.

⚙ WALL FIXTURE. 1 light with a fluted socket cover on a curved arm with a cast, scrolled terminal; solid brass; several finishes. 5" wide, 8" high, extends 13", 2¼" shade fitter. No. W-605.

⚙ WALL FIXTURE. 1 light with a fluted socket cover on a cast, classical arm extending from an oval back plate;

WALL FIXTURE. No. W-660. Victorian Lightcrafters.

solid brass; several finishes. 5″ wide, 9″ high, extends 8″, 4⅛″ x 6″ oval wall plate, 2¼″ shade fitter. No. W-660.

✪ WALL FIXTURE. 1 light suspended from a Classical Revival scroll; solid brass; several finishes. 5″ wide, 11″ high, extends 12″, 2¼″ shade fitter. No. W-851.

✪ WALL FIXTURE. 1 light arching from a classical wall plate; solid brass; several finishes. 5″ wide, 13″ high, extends 12″, 3¼″ shade fitter. No. W-920.

✪ WALL FIXTURE. 1 light suspended from a reeded classical rod; solid brass; several finishes. 5″ wide, 11″ high, extends 8″, 2¼″ shade fitter. No. W-975.

✪ WALL FIXTURE. 3 lights suspended from a Classical Revival rod; solid brass; several finishes. 21″ wide, 11″ high, extends 8″, 2¼″ shade fitter. No. W-975-3.

VICTORIAN LIGHTING WORKS

✪ WALL BRACKETS. 3 in brass with 1 or 2 lights. Turn-of-the-century look. Not based on specific documents.

VICTORIAN REPRODUCTION LIGHTING COMPANY

✪ WALL BRACKETS. 8 fixtures in brass (7 with 1 light, 1 with 2 lights). Turn-of-the-century look. Not based on specific documents.

D'LIGHTS

✪ ART DECO SIDELIGHTS. 3 fixtures. Adaptations.

METROPOLITAN LIGHTING FIXTURE COMPANY

✪ ART DECO SIDELIGHTS. Numerous fixtures. Adaptations.

REJUVENATION LAMP AND FIXTURE COMPANY

✪ ALSEA. Craftsman-style porch bracket with 1 light; cast iron; black enamel finish. Early 20th century. 6″ wide, 12″ high, extends 8″, 6″ ball shade with 3¼″ fitter. UL listed for damp locations. Reproduction of a document in manufacturer's collection. No. WPCA.

✪ COTTAGE GROVE. Mission style with 2 lights; brass; several finishes. Early 20th century. 17″ wide, 10″ high, extends 9″, 1¼″ shade fitters. Adaptation of a document in manufacturer's collection. No. WY2E.

✪ MANZANITA. Mission style with 1 light; brass; sev-

ELECTRIC WALL BRACKETS: 20TH CENTURY

ALSEA. Rejuvenation Lamp and Fixture Company.

eral finishes. Early 20th century. 6″ wide, 9″ high, extends 10″, 2¼″ shade fitter. Adaptation of a document in manufacturer's collection. No. WY1E.

RENAISSANCE MARKETING

✿ FLORAL SCONCES. 6 Art Nouveau fixtures with a cluster of 1–7 floral stems; cast bronze patinated with a Tiffany-style green brown finish; silver lustre art glass shades. Adaptation.

MANZANITA. Rejuvenation Lamp and Fixture Company.

THE RENOVATOR'S SUPPLY

✿ ART DECO SIDELIGHTS. 7 in alabaster, polished brass or ribbed glass. c. 1930 look. Not based on specific documents. Alabaster series ("Lido," 13″ wide; "Collette," 9¾″ wide) is suitable for Art Deco theater renovations. Alastair Duncan, *Art Nouveau and Art Deco Lighting*.

FLORAL SCONCES. Renaissance Marketing.

CLASSIC ILLUMINATION

✪ BOWL LIGHT. Bowl hung from rods; solid brass; various finishes. 10″–16″ wide depending on shade, various lengths. No. 1920.

M-H LAMP AND FAN COMPANY

✪ BOWL-STYLE CHANDELIER. Molded bowl suspended from 3 brass chains. 14″ wide, min. length 18″, standard length 27″. No. 8345.

✪ BOWL-STYLE CHANDELIER. Molded bowl suspended from 3 brass chains surrounded by 3 pendant lights. 22½″ wide, min. length 18″, standard length 27″. No. 8346.

REJUVENATION LAMP AND FIXTURE COMPANY

✪ LADD'S ADDITION. Bowl suspended from rods. Early 20th century. 14″ wide, min. length 22″, standard

BOWL LIGHTS: 20TH CENTURY

below left
LADD'S ADDITION. Rejuvenation Lamp and Fixture Company.

below right
LAURELHURST. Rejuvenation Lamp and Fixture Company.

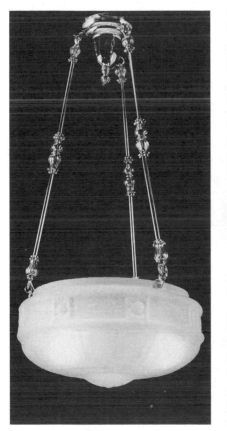

BOWL FIXTURE. No. EC3-8. Roy Electric Company.

length 30". Adaptation of a common form. No. CDB.

✸ LAURELHURST. Bowl suspended from chains. Early 20th century. 14" wide, min. length 24", standard length 24". Gold plastic lamp cord for UL listing; available with cloth lamp cord by special order. Adaptation of a common form. No. CHB.

ROY ELECTRIC COMPANY

✸ BOWL FIXTURE. Rod-hung bowl surrounded by 7 pendant lights with cast arms. c. 1920. 29" wide, 24" high. No. EC3-8.

CEILING LIGHTS: 20TH CENTURY

CLASSIC ILLUMINATION

✸ PAN FIXTURE. Classical Revival with etched-glass shade. 12" wide, 8" high. No. 1921.

✸ SURFACE-MOUNTED FIXTURE. Lalique-style French Art Deco shade. 13" wide, 14" high. No. 1924.

D'LIGHTS

❂ FLUSHMOUNTS. 9 fixtures. Early 20th century. Adaptations.

M-H LAMP AND FAN COMPANY

❂ CEILING FIXTURE. Surface-mounted pan fixture with 3 sockets. 18″ wide, 8″ long, 2¼″ shade fitter. No. 8326.

❂ CEILING FIXTURE. Flush-mounted fixture to hold opal shade. 8″ wide, 8½″ long, 4″ shade fitter; 12″ wide shade. Adaptation of typical pre–World War II kitchen and institutional fixtures. No. 8329.

REJUVENATION LAMP AND FIXTURE COMPANY

❂ MOUNT TABOR. Flush-mounted ceiling fixture with 2, 3, 4 or 5 lights suspended from chain links. Early 20th century. 18″ wide, 10″ long, 2¼″ shade fitter. Adaptation of a common form. No. CTE.

❂ PORCH LIGHT. Ceiling mounted with enclosed glass shade. 20th century. 8″ wide, 12″ long. UL listed for damp locations. Reproduction of a document in manufacturer's collection. No. CK4-EX.

VICTORIAN REPRODUCTION LIGHTING COMPANY

❂ CEILING LIGHTS. 3 in brass. Early 20th-century look. Not based on specific documents.

above left
SURFACE-MOUNTED FIXTURE. No. 1924. Classic Illumination.

above right
PORCH LIGHT. No. CK4-EX. Rejuvenation Lamp and Fixture Company.

SPECIALTY ITEMS
AND SERVICES

In addition to the manufacturers of reproduction light-ing fixtures, numerous companies and dealers offer special lighting products and services of interest to owners of historic buildings. For addresses, see the suppliers list.

Ideally, the shops below that specialize in lighting antiques should be visited in person (call first for an appointment), but most dealers will accept inquiries by mail and will send photographs of lamps and fixtures in their stock. When corresponding with these dealers it is helpful to include an illustration of the lighting device being sought—a photocopy from one of the books listed in the bibliography, perhaps—and a self-addressed, stamped envelope.

ANTIQUE
LIGHTING
FIXTURES

ART DIRECTIONS
AUTHENTIC LIGHTING
JOAN BOGART
BRASS KNOB
BRASS MENAGERIE
CENTURY HOUSE ANTIQUES
CITY BARN ANTIQUES
CITY LIGHTS
JEFFREY DAVIS AND COMPANY
SAMUEL J. DORNSIFE
GREG'S ANTIQUE LIGHTING
HEXAGRAM
ILLUSTRIOUS LIGHTING
JOHN KRUESEL'S GENERAL MERCHANDISE
LITTLEWOOD AND MAUE
LONDON VENTURES COMPANY

CUSTOM LANTERN.
Mill River
Hammerworks.

CANDLES

MATERIALS UNLIMITED
C. NERI ANTIQUES
OLD LAMPLIGHTER SHOP
OLD WORLD ANTIQUES
RESTORED ANTIQUE LIGHTING
RIVERWALK LIGHTING AND GIFTS
ROY ELECTRIC COMPANY
STANLEY GALLERIES
YANKEE CRAFTSMAN

CANDLES

ELCANCO

The leading firm offering handcrafted electric wax "candles" and flamelike bulbs.

❂ CANDLE COVERS. Hand-dipped beeswax candle covers to slip over existing wiring; gold or ivory. ⁷⁄₈" or 1¹⁄₄" diameter, custom lengths. Suitable as replacements for plastic "candles" supplied with many electrified fixtures.

❂ LOW-VOLTAGE ADAPTERS. 6 inexpensive adapters to reduce normal household voltage (110–130 volts) to 6 volts. Supply up to 20 low-voltage candles. Plug into a wall outlet or may be permanently installed. Larger-capacity models available by special order.

❂ MORELITE BULBS. Small, screw-base bulbs fit Elcanco "Morelite" electric wax candles; clear or frosted. 7¹⁄₂, 15 or 25 watts. Operate on normal household voltage. Installed at the John Brown House, Providence, R.I.

❂ MORELITE ELECTRIC WAX CANDLES. Resemble authentic beeswax candles; wired to accept the "Morelite" bulb; gold or ivory. ⁷⁄₈" diameter, 2"–12" high. Wired with 5 feet of gold, clear or black wire; longer lengths available. Instructions for wiring supplied. Operate on normal household voltage.

❂ STARLITE CANDLEWICK BULBS. Tiny, screw-base, 1-candlepower bulbs fit Elcanco "Starlite" electric wax candles. Life expectancy 5,000 hours. Require low-voltage adapter. Installed at Mount Vernon, Gunston Hall, Gore Place, Colonial Williamsburg and Historic Deerfield.

❂ STARLITE ELECTRIC WAX CANDLES. Resemble authentic beeswax candles; wired to accept the "Starlite"

MORELITE ELECTRIC WAX CANDLE. Clear, 7-watts. Elcano.

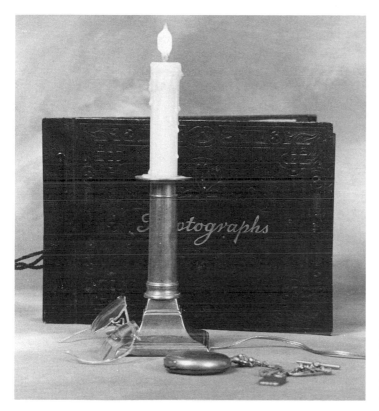

STARLITE ELECTRIC
WAX CANDLE.
Antique candleholder.
Elcano.

bulb; gold or ivory. ⅛" diameter, 2"–12" high. Wired with 5 feet of gold, clear or black wire; longer lengths available. Instructions for wiring supplied. Operate on low voltage only. Installed at Mount Vernon, Gunston Hall, Gore Place, Colonial Williamsburg and Historic Deerfield.

CRYSTAL PRISMS

CRYSTAL MOUNTAIN PRISMS

Numerous glass prisms, pendants, chains, bobeches and drops to replace missing or damaged originals.

LUIGI CRYSTAL

Small line of crystal prisms and bobeches to replace missing or damaged originals.

R. WILKINSON AND SON

Holder of the Royal Warrant as glass restorers to Queen Elizabeth II. Offers numerous antique and reproduction arms, prisms, chains and related items to restore glass chandeliers and other lighting devices.

CUSTOM
MANUFACTURERS

Many of the firms listed throughout this book restore or reproduce lighting fixtures. The firms listed below, however, specialize in custom orders.

SAMUEL J. DORNSIFE

Consultant in historic lighting and supplier of custom-made reproductions of 19th-century fixtures for museums and historic houses.

KAYNE AND SON

Custom-forged hardware and lighting fixtures in the colonial style.

LITTLEWOOD AND MAUE

Consultants in historic lighting and suppliers of custom-made reproductions of early 19th-century lighting for museums and historic houses, including blown-glass shades and chimneys for Argand-burner fixtures.

THOMAS LOOSE

Custom-forged hardware and lighting fixtures in the colonial style.

MILL RIVER HAMMERWORKS

Custom forging, spinning and casting; specializes in lanterns and chandeliers fitted for candles.

RAMBUSCH COMPANY

Custom lighting fixtures, stained glass, interior restorations, art metalwork, liturgical consulting, painting and decorating, murals, mosaics and sculpture in all materials.

WASHINGTON COPPER WORKS

Custom-fashioned copper lanterns, ceiling fixtures, chandeliers and sconces fitted for candles or electricity.

ELECTRIC LIGHT
BULBS

BRADFORD CONSULTANTS

Manufacturers' representative selling Kyp-Go lamps listed

below and other specialty lamps of use to owners of historic buildings.

KYP-GO

⊙ CENTURY. Electric light bulb with hairpin carbon filament in clear-tip bulb; fits modern medium-size screw base. 120 volts. Late 19th century. 6″ high. Based on an early Edison bulb.

⊙ EDISON-STYLE CARBON-FILAMENT BULBS. 2 sizes with looped-carbon filaments in clear-tip bulbs to fit modern medium-size screw bases. 120 volts. Early 20th century. "Bijou": 8 candlepower, 2³⁄₈″ diameter. "Imperial": 16 candlepower, 2³⁄₈″ diameter. Suitable for fixtures predating tungsten filament (1907–11).

⊙ EUREKA BULBS. 2 styles with zigzag tungsten filaments in clear bulbs; fit modern medium-size screw bases. 120 volts. 1909. Based on the General Electric Mazda incandescent bulb. "T" type: for 1909–20 (tip bulb). "P" type: for 1920–30 (tipless bulb). 60 watts of brilliant white light. Not suitable for exposed installations; can be used with dimmer.

CLASSIC ACCENTS

ELECTRIC PUSH-BUTTON LIGHT SWITCHES AND PLATES

⊙ PUSH-BUTTON LIGHT SWITCHES. Single-station and 3-way switch styles. 110 volts, 15 amps. No. S-90 (single station); No. S-93W (3-way).

⊙ PUSH-BUTTON LIGHT-SWITCH PLATES. Polished brass, ivory and dark brown styles for single- and multiple-button switches.

SACO MANUFACTURING AND WOODWORKING COMPANY

LAMP POSTS: WOODEN EXTERIOR

Nine posts for mounting exterior residential lanterns. Kiln-dried Eastern white pine with round, tapered, square, octagonal or turned sections. 8′ high, 4½″ base; custom heights to 18′. One end turned to accept a 3″ lamp base. Bored for wiring.

Most of the manufacturers here offer fabric shades in a wide variety of styles and sizes appropriate for the period 1890–1920. Because all the firms produce each shade by hand around a metal stiffening frame, it is possible to

LAMP SHADES: FABRIC AND PAPER

request a custom re-covering adapted from one of their designs using an antique shade frame. Submit photographs and dimensions for a price quotation.

BURDOCH SILK LAMPSHADE COMPANY

Line of 15 handsewn and embroidered late Victorian and Edwardian fabric shades for electric lamps and hanging fixtures.

LITTLEWOOD AND MAUE

Custom-order paper shades for mid-19th-century solar lamps.

SHADES OF THE PAST

Line of 16 silk, fringed turn-of-the-century shades for electric lamps and wall brackets.

THE SHADE TREE

Cut and pierced parchment paper shades for lamps; particularly useful small (3″ x 4″, 3″ x 5″) "flame shades" for early 20th-century electrified hanging fixtures and sconces.

YESTERSHADES

Numerous turn-of-the-century fabric shades for electric lamps and hanging fixtures.

LAMP SHADES AND CHIMNEYS: GLASS

Most manufacturers of gas, gas-electric and electric fixtures offer a variety of glass shades to fit their fixtures that may be ordered separately as replacements or for use on antique fixtures. The firms listed here have extensive lines or offer shades and chimneys not readily available. Check dimensions carefully before ordering.

B AND P LAMP SUPPLY

Numerous handblown and decorated shades for kerosene, gas and electric fixtures; glass chimneys.

CLASSIC ILLUMINATION

Shades particularly useful for 20th-century electric fixtures.

FAIRE HARBOUR

Glass shades, chimneys and mantles for kerosene lamps.

HOLOPHANE

Holophane glass shades for 20th-century hanging fixtures.

LITTLEWOOD AND MAUE

Small but important line of handblown and cut-glass shades and chimneys for Argand-burner fixtures, including solar lamps.

LUNDBERG STUDIOS

Quality line of late Victorian, Art Nouveau and Art Deco glass shades.

SOLAR GLOBE. $9^{3}/_{4}$" high. Littlewood and Maue.

right
ARGAND-BURNER
GLOBE. 7⅝″ high. Lit-
tlewood and Maue.

below
ART NOUVEAU and
ART DECO GLASS
SHADES. Lundberg
Studios.

M-H LAMP AND FAN COMPANY
Late 19th- and early 20th-century gas and electric fixture shades.

PAXTON HARDWARE
Handblown, painted and etched-glass shades for late 19th-century gas, electric and kerosene fixtures and lamps; glass chimneys for kerosene lamps.

REJUVENATION LAMP AND FIXTURE COMPANY
Shades for late gas-electric fixtures.

RENAISSANCE MARKETING
Numerous art glass shades for electric fixtures.

VICTORIAN REPRODUCTION LIGHTING
Numerous late 19th- and 20th-century glass shades.

GOLDEN AGE GLASSWORKS
Restoration and manufacture of stained-glass windows and leaded lamp shades; custom shade reproductions.

LYN HOVEY STUDIO
Superior line of lamp shades inspired by turn-of-the-century Art Nouveau designs. Although appropriate for a traditional interior, each shade is an original design rather than a line-for-line copy.

SCHLITZ STUDIOS
High-quality leaded-glass shades, windows and mosaics from custom designs; extensive line of reproduction Tiffany shades.

TIFFANY DESIGN LAMPS
Numerous Tiffany-style lamp shades; 75 kits for those who wish to assemble their own shades.

LAMP SHADES: LEADED GLASS

STREET LIGHTING

The rapid growth of Main Street and other preservation activities and the creation of urban historic districts have created a demand for reproduction street lamps. Several firms offer such lighting in a variety of historical styles and materials—cast iron, bronze, aluminum, steel and fiberglass. A community should select the post and luminaire (lamp) designs that most closely match originals or a style from the street's dominant period.

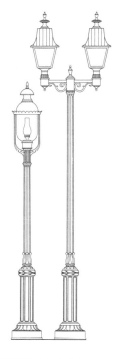

ANTIQUE STREET LAMPS

❂ POSTS AND LUMINAIRES. Numerous posts in cast iron, cast iron and steel, fiberglass-reinforced polyester, cast aluminum and polysteel, with various luminaires. Late 19th to early 20th century. 6½′–21′ high. Adaptations of period gas and electrical designs.

DUTCH PRODUCTS AND SUPPLY COMPANY

❂ POSTS AND LUMINAIRES. Imported products by Kes Schouten of Holland. Late 19th to early 20th century. Adaptations of European designs.

LAMPCO

❂ POSTS AND LUMINAIRES. 6 posts and 8 luminaires. 20th century.

LAMP LIGHT INDUSTRIES

❂ ORIGINAL POSTS. Reconditioned cast iron. 1920s.

MAINSTREET LIGHTING STANDARDS

❂ POSTS. Fiberglass and aluminum. Late 19th to early 20th century. Adaptations of cast-iron designs.

CAST-IRON POSTS. Central Park Series. Antique Street Lamps.

opposite
Salina Street, Syracuse, N.Y., c. 1916, lighted with streetlights (No. 5, now No. 1355) by Union Metal Corporation

far right
BOROUGH POST and
LUMINAIRE. Spring
City Electrical Manu-
facturing Company.

right
BISHOP'S CROOK
POST and LUMINAIRE.
Spring City Electrical
Manufacturing
Company.

NOSTALGIA

⊛ POLES AND LANTERNS. Imported cast-aluminum
poles and copper lanterns by the Victorian Lamp Manufacturing Company of England. Adaptations of Victorian
designs.

RWL/WELSBACH LIGHTING

⊛ POSTS AND LUMINAIRES. Cast-iron or aluminum
posts with interchangeable bases, brackets, ladder rests
and luminaires. 1877 to late 19th century. Documents in
manufacturer's collection. Suitable for street and public
building gaslight installations where complete documentation is not available.

SPRING CITY ELECTRICAL MANUFACTURING COMPANY

⊛ BISHOP'S CROOK. Fluted cast-iron post arched over

far left
FRANKLIN POST. Society Hill luminaire. Spring City Electrical Manufacturing Company.

left
HARRISBURG POST and LUMINAIRE. Spring City Electrical Manufacturing Company.

suspended electric luminaire. New York City, c. 1892. Reproduction. 20'–23' 10¾" high, 21" round base.

⊙ BOROUGH. Spiral-turned, cast-iron gaslight post. c. 1880s. Reproduction. 8½'–10' high, exclusive of luminaire; 11½"–14" octagonal base.

⊙ BROOKLYN. Round cast-iron electric post. New York City, 1883. Reproduction of the Brooklyn Bridge post originally used for electric carbon-arc lights. 10' high, exclusive of luminaire; 16" x 22" octagonal base.

⊙ FRANKLIN. Square cast-iron post. Philadelphia, c. 1751. Replica of a cedar post probably made for use with a whale-oil lamp designed by Benjamin Franklin. 8'9½"–12' high, exclusive of luminaire. Installed in Society Hill, Philadelphia.

⊙ HANCOCK. Round, fluted cast-iron gaslight post. Boston, c. 1860. Reproduction of a post used extensively in Boston. 9'–13' high, exclusive of luminaire; 16" round base.

MADISON POST. Harrisburg luminaire. Spring City Electrical Manufacturing Company.

opposite top
SEA WALL POST and LUMINAIRE. No. 3092. Installed at Lakeland, Fla., 1927. Union Metal Corporation.

opposite bottom
No. 653 POST and LUMINAIRE. San Antonio, Tex., downtown, c. 1920s. Union Metal Corporation.

◉ HARRISBURG. Narrow, round cast-iron electric post. 1901. Reproduction of a post designed by New York architect Arnold Brunner. 11'–12½' high, exclusive of luminaire; 20½" octagonal base.

◉ INDEPENDENCE. Fluted cast-iron post. Late colonial. Replica of a wooden post installed at Independence National Historical Park, Philadelphia. 7¼' high, exclusive of luminaire; 12" square base.

◉ MADISON. Round cast-iron electric post. New York City, 1907. Reproduction of a post designed by architect Henry Bacon for Central Park, New York City. 7¼'–13½' high, exclusive of luminaire; 18½" round base.

◉ NEWBURYPORT. Cast-iron gaslight post. c. 1850–60. Reproduction of a post used extensively in New England. 9'10", 12' or 13' high, exclusive of luminaire; 13"–16" square base.

◉ PRINCETON. Cast-iron gaslight post. Pre-1850. Reproduction of one of the earliest documented gaslight posts. 9'–11' high, exclusive of luminaire; 12" square base.

◉ VILLA. Round cast-iron electric post. c. 1900–15. Reproduction. 10' to 12'11" high, exclusive of luminaire; 17"–21" round base.

◉ WASHINGTON. Fluted cast-iron electric post. Washington, D.C., 1910. Reproduction of a post designed for the U.S. Commission of Fine Arts. 10' to 18'11" high, exclusive of luminaire; 17"–25" round and octagonal bases.

◉ WINCHESTER. Square cast-iron electric post. Kentucky, 1913. Reproduction of a post designed by James Love, a Winchester, Ky., foundry man, and used originally in Winchester, Louisville and Frankfort, Ky. 10'1" high, exclusive of luminaire; 16⅜" square base.

UNION METAL CORPORATION

◉ POSTS. Concrete or sheet steel with cast-iron base. 1906–30s. Documents in manufacturer's collection.

Union Metal Lighting Standards
Design No. 3097
Sea Wall & Civic Center,
Lakeland, Fla
4-L-302

Union Metal Lamp Standards
Design No 653
San Antonio, Texas

APPENDIX

SUPPLIERS

Listed below are the full name, address and telephone number of each firm mentioned in this book. With few exceptions, manufacturers will sell directly to the consumer. Most provide illustrated catalogs for a modest charge.

A. J. P., COPPERSMITH AND COMPANY. 20 Industrial Parkway, Woburn, Mass. 01801 (617) 245-1223.

ANTIQUE STREET LAMPS. 8412 South Congress Avenue, P.O. Box 43289, Austin, Tex. 78745-5675 (512) 282-9780

ARROYO CRAFTSMAN. 127 East St. Joseph Street, Suite 101, Arcadia, Calif. 91006 (818) 574-3930

ART DIRECTIONS. 6120 Delmar Boulevard, St. Louis, Mo. 63112 (314) 863-1895

AUTHENTIC DESIGNS. Mill Road, West Rupert, Vt. 05776-0011 (802) 394-7713

AUTHENTIC LIGHTING. 558 Grand Avenue, Englewood, N.J. 07631 (201) 568-7429

BALDWIN HARDWARE MANUFACTURING COMPANY. 841 Wyomissing Boulevard, Reading, Pa. 19611 (215) 777-7811

BALL AND BALL. 463 West Lincoln Highway, Exton, Pa. 19341 (215) 363-7330

B AND P LAMP SUPPLY COMPANY. Route 3, McMinnville, Tenn. 37110 (615) 473-3016

LESTER H. BERRY AND COMPANY. P.O. Box 53377, Philadelphia, Pa. 19105 (215) 923-2603

JOAN BOGART. 1392 Old North Boulevard, Roslyn, N.Y. 11576 (516) 621-2454

BRADFORD CONSULTANTS. P.O. Box 4020, Alameda, Calif. 94501 (415) 523-1968

BRASS KNOB. 2311 18th Street, N.W., Washington, D.C. 20009 (202) 332-3370

BRASSLIGHT. 90 Main Street, Nyack, N.Y. 10960 (914) 353-0567

BRASS MENAGERIE. 524 St. Louis Street, New Orleans, La. 70130 (504) 524-0921

BURDOCH SILK LAMPSHADE COMPANY. 1145 Industrial Avenue, Escondido, Calif. 92025 (619) 745-3275

CENTURY HOUSE ANTIQUES. 46785 Route 18, Wellington, Ohio 44090 (216) 647-4092

CITY BARN ANTIQUES. 362 Atlantic Avenue, Brooklyn, N.Y. 11217 (718) 855-8566

CITY LIGHTS. 2226 Massachusetts Avenue, Cambridge, Mass. 02140 (617) 547-1490

CLASSIC ACCENTS. P.O. Box 1181, Southgate, Mich. 48195 (313) 282-5523

CLASSIC ILLUMINATION. 2743 Ninth Street, Berkeley, Calif. 94710 (415) 849-1842

COLONIAL METALCRAFTERS. P.O. Box 1135, Tyler, Tex. 75710 (214) 561-1111

COPPER HOUSE Division of W. L. Smith Company, R.F.D. 1, Box 4, Epsom, N.H. 03234 (603) 736-9798

JOSIAH R. COPPERSMYTHE. 80 Stiles Road, Boylston, Mass. 01505 (617) 869-2769

CRYSTAL MOUNTAIN PRISMS. P.O. Box 31, Westfield, N.Y. 14787 (716) 326-3676

JEFFREY DAVIS AND COMPANY. 37 Presidio Avenue, San Francisco, Calif. 94115 (415) 921-1200

D'LIGHTS. 533 West Windsor Road, Glendale, Calif. 91204-1891 (818) 956-5656

SAMUEL J. DORNSIFE. 974 Hollywood Circle, Williamsport, Pa. 17701 (717) 322-1550

DUTCH PRODUCTS AND SUPPLY COMPANY. 166 Lincoln Avenue, Yardley, Pa. 19067 (215) 493-4873

ELCANCO. 40 Beharell Street, West Concord, Mass. 01742 (617) 256-4483

ESSEX FORGE. 1 Old Dennison Road, Essex, Conn. 06426 (203) 767-1808

FAIRE HARBOUR. 44 Captain Peirce Road, Scituate,

Mass. 02066 (617) 545-2465

GATES MOORE. River Road, Silvermine, R.D. 3, Norwalk, Conn. 06850 (203) 847-3231

GOLDEN AGE GLASSWORKS. 339 Bellvale Road, Warwick, N.Y. 10990 (914) 986-1487

GREG'S ANTIQUE LIGHTING. 12005 Wilshire Boulevard, West Los Angeles, Calif. 90025 (213) 478-5475

PAUL HANSON. 610 Commercial Avenue, Carlstadt, N.J. 07072 (201) 933-4873

HERITAGE LANTERNS. 70A Main Street, Yarmouth, Maine 04096 (207) 846-3911

HEXAGRAM. 2247 Rohnerville Road, Fortuna, Calif. 95540 (707) 725-6223

HOLOPHANE. 214 Oakwood Avenue, Newark, Ohio 43055 (303) 978-4900

LYN HOVEY STUDIO. 266 Concord Avenue, Cambridge, Mass. 02138 (617) 492-6566

HURLEY PATENTEE LIGHTING. R.D. 7, P.O. Box 98A, Kingston, N.Y. 12401 (914) 331-5414

ILLUSTRIOUS LIGHTING. 1925 Fillmore Street, San Francisco, Calif. 94115 (415) 922-3133

KAYNE AND SON CUSTOM FORGED HARDWARE. 76 Daniel Ridge Road, Candler, N.C. 28715 (704) 667-8868

KING'S CHANDELIER COMPANY. Highway 14, P.O. Box 667, Eden, N.C. 27288 (919) 623-6188

JOHN KRUESEL'S GENERAL MERCHANDISE. 22 Southwest Third Street, Rochester, Minn. 55901 (507) 289-8049

KYP-GO. P.O. Box 247, St. Charles, Ill. 60174 (312) 584-8181

LAMPCO. 2214 Denison Avenue, Cleveland, Ohio 44109 (216) 351-9110

LAMP LIGHT INDUSTRIES. 135 Yorkshire Court, Elyria, Ohio 44035 (216) 365-4954

LIGHTING BY HAMMERWORKS. 6 Fremont Street, Worcester, Mass. 01603 (617) 755-3434

LITTLEWOOD AND MAUE. P.O. Box 402, Palmyra, N.J. 08065 (609) 829-4615

LONDON VENTURES COMPANY. 2 Dock Square, Rockport, Mass. 01966 (617) 546-7161

THOMAS LOOSE. Blacksmith/Whitesmith, R.D. 2, P.O.

Box 2410, Leesport, Pa. 19533 (215) 926-4849

LUIGI CRYSTAL. 7332 Frankford Avenue, Philadelphia, Pa. 19136 (215) 338-2978

LUNDBERG STUDIOS. 131 Marine View Avenue, P.O. Box C, Davenport, Calif. 95017 (408) 423-2532

MAINSTREET LIGHTING STANDARDS. 11020 Berea Road, Cleveland, Ohio 44102 (216) 651-4431

MATERIALS UNLIMITED. 2 West Michigan Avenue, Ypsilanti, Mich. 48197 (313) 483-6980

METROPOLITAN LIGHTING FIXTURE COMPANY. 315 East 62nd Street, New York, N.Y. 10021 (212) 838-2425

M-H LAMP AND FAN COMPANY. 7231½ North Sheridan Road, Chicago, Ill. 60626

MILL RIVER HAMMERWORKS. 65 Canal Street, Turners Falls, Mass. 01376 (413) 863-8388

C. NERI ANTIQUES. 313 South Street, Philadelphia, Pa. 19147 (215) 923-6669

NOSTALGIA. 307 Stiles Avenue, Savannah, Ga. 31401 (912) 236-8176

NOWELL'S. P.O. Box 295, Sausalito, Calif. 94966 (415) 332-4933

OLD LAMPLIGHTER SHOP. Musical Museum, Deansboro, N.Y. 13328 (315) 841-8774

OLD WORLD ANTIQUES. 1715 Summit, Kansas City, Mo. 64108 (816) 472-0815

PAXTON HARDWARE. 7818 Bradshaw Road, Upper Falls, Md. 21156 (301) 592-8505

PERIOD LIGHTING FIXTURES. 1 West Main Street, Chester, Conn. 06412 (203) 526-3690

PRICE GLOVER. 817½ Madison Avenue, New York, N.Y. 10021 (212) 772-1740

PROGRESS LIGHTING. Consult your local Progress distributor (found in the Yellow Pages) or telephone (215) 289-1200

RAMBUSCH COMPANY. 40 West 13th Street, New York, N.Y. 10011 (212) 675-0400

REJUVENATION LAMP AND FIXTURE COMPANY. 901 North Skidmore, Portland, Ore. 97217 (503) 249-0774

RENAISSANCE MARKETING. P.O. Box 360, Lake Orion, Mich. 48035 (313) 693-1109

THE RENOVATOR'S SUPPLY. Millers Falls, Mass. 01349 (413) 659-2211

RESTORED ANTIQUE LIGHTING. P.O. Box 141, Fair Haven, N.J. 07701 (201) 842-7377

RIVERWALK LIGHTING AND GIFTS. 401 South Main Street, Naperville, Ill. 60540 (312) 357-0200

ROY ELECTRIC COMPANY. 1054 Coney Island Avenue, Brooklyn, N.Y. 11230 (718) 339-6311

RWL/WELSBACH LIGHTING. 240 Sargent Drive, New Haven, Conn. 06511 (203) 789-1710

SACO MANUFACTURING AND WOODWORKING. 39 Lincoln Street, Saco, Maine 04072 (207) 284-6613

THE SALT BOX. 3004 Columbia Avenue, Lancaster, Pa. 17603 (717) 392-5649

ST. LOUIS ANTIQUE LIGHTING COMPANY. 801 North Skinker, St. Louis, Mo. 63130 (314) 863-1414

SCHLITZ STUDIOS. 245 North Water Street, Milwaukee, Wis. 53202 (414) 277-0742

SHADES OF THE PAST. P.O. Box 502, Corte Madera, Calif. 94925 (415) 459-6999

THE SHADE TREE. Gail Teller, 6 Half-King Drive, Burlington, Conn. 06013 (203) 673-9358

WILLIAM SPENCER. Creek Road, Rancocas Woods, N.J. 08060 (609) 235-1830

SPRING CITY ELECTRICAL MANUFACTURING COMPANY. P.O. Drawer A, Hall and Main Streets, Spring City, Pa. 19475-0030 (215) 948-4000

STANLEY GALLERIES. 2118 North Clark Street, Chicago, Ill. 60614 (312) 281-1614

TIFFANY DESIGN LAMPS. P.O. Box 71895, Las Vegas, Nev. 89170-1895 (702) 645-5547

UNION METAL CORPORATION. P.O. Box 9920, Canton, Ohio 44711 (216) 456-7653

VICTORIAN LIGHTCRAFTERS. P.O. Box 350, Slate Hill, N.Y. 10973 (914) 355-1300

VICTORIAN LIGHTING WORKS. 251 Pennsylvania Avenue, P.O. Box 469, Centre Hall, Pa. 16828 (814) 364-9577

VICTORIAN REPRODUCTION LIGHTING COMPANY. 1601 Park Avenue, South, Minneapolis, Minn. 55404 (612) 338-3636

VIRGINIA METALCRAFTERS. 1010 East Main Street, P.O. Box 1068, Waynesboro, Va. 22980 (703) 949-8205

E. G. WASHBURNE AND COMPANY. 85 Andover Street, Danvers, Mass. 01923 (617) 774-3645

WASHINGTON COPPER WORKS. 49 South Street, Washington, Conn. 06793 (203) 868-7527

R. WILKINSON AND SON. 43–45 Wastdale Road, London SE 23 1HN, England (01-699-4420)

LT. MOSES WILLARD. 1156 U.S. Route 50, Milford, Ohio 45150 (513) 831-8956

WINDY LANE FLUORESCENTS. 35972 Highway 6, Hillrose, Colo. 80733 (303) 847-3710

YANKEE CRAFTSMAN. 357 Commonwealth Road, Wayland, Mass. 01778 (617) 653-0031

YESTERSHADES. 3824 Southeast Stark, Portland, Ore. 97214 (503) 238-5755

ADAPTATION. A modern fixture retaining the overall but not exact appearance of a document (original) or several closely related documents. Also, fixtures produced as companions to a reproduction; for example, wall brackets that match a gaselier reproduced from a document.

ANNULAR LAMP. Astral, sinumbra and certain other lamps of the first half of the 19th century whose fuel reservoirs were formed in a hollow ring, designed to reduce the shadow cast by the offset reservoir typically used in early Argand-burner lamps.

ARGAND BURNER. A lamp burner fueled by whale or colza oil that generated more light than several candles, was adjustable and did not require constant tending. A tubular wick within a cylinder permitted a current of air to flow through the burner, increasing combustion and the resulting light. The burner was named for François-Pierre Ami Argand (1750–1803), the Swiss-born chemist working in France who is generally considered the inventor of this first scientific lighting device about 1783. One drawback was that the offset oil reservoir, located to one side of the burner, cast a shadow.

ASTRAL LAMP. A 19th-century lamp that used an Argand burner set in the middle of an annular fuel reservoir, which reduced the shadow cast by the offset reservoir of the early Argand-type lamps. Patented by Bordier-Marcet in 1809, it was named "astral" because the light came from above like stars (from the French, *astral*, meaning starry). *See also* sinumbra lamp.

BATSWING BURNER. Invented in England about 1816, this gas burner created an efficient, flat flame. It was an improvement over the earliest open-tube (ratstail) gas burners and was formed by cutting a thin slot in a domed tip. In the 1850s the burners were provided with soapstone tips that would not corrode.

BAYBERRY WAX. Slow-burning candle wax rendered from berries of the bayberry shrub, *Myrica cerifera*.

BOBECHE. A glass or metal disk, cast as part of the candleholder or detachable, to capture melting wax.

BOWL LIGHT. A popular form of electric hanging fixture of the 1910–20 period. An opaque glass bowl hid the light bulbs and provided an indirect light source.

BURNING FLUID. A mixture of alcohol and turpentine with other ingredients. Used for lamp fuel, mainly in the 1830s–60s, it provided a clean flame and flowed easily up a wick but was dangerously explosive.

CAMPHENE. Freshly distilled turpentine used as a lamp fuel.

CANDELABRUM. A branched holder for candles designed to sit on a table, pedestal, bracket or mantel.

CANDLESTICK. A portable holder for a single candle, made of diverse materials including wood, pewter, brass, iron, silver and glass.

CHANDELIER. A decorative holder for candles that is hung from the ceiling.

COLZA OIL. Lamp fuel extracted from the seeds of *Brassica napus*, a member of the cabbage family. Used mainly in Europe as an alternative to whale oil, it was also known as rape seed oil.

DOCUMENT. An original lighting fixture copied for a reproduction or an adaptation.

DOUTER. A scissorlike implement with each blade terminating in a metal disc to pinch and extinguish a candle flame—thus, a "do outer." Not to be confused with an extinguisher or snuffer.

ELECTROLIER. An electric chandelier.

EXTINGUISHER. A conical device made of metal with a handle for extinguishing a candle flame.

FISHTAIL BURNER. A gas burner with holes in the tip developed in England about 1820. The resulting flame formed the fishtail shape that gave the burner its name.

FONT. A container for fuel in a lighting fixture.

GADROON. Fluted or reeded ornament, e.g., on a chandelier.

GASELIER. An ornamental frame or chandelier holding a number of gas burners that is hung from the ceiling; variously spelled "gasalier" and "gasolier." The term came into general use in the 1840s, replacing the previously used "gas chandelier." When electric lights were added to such fixtures in the late 19th century, the fixtures often were called "gaselier-electroliers."

GASLIGHT. A distillate of coal used for street lighting in the early 19th century and used widely for residential lighting in large cities from the 1830s to the 1920s. Not to be confused with natural gas.

GAS LIGHTER. A device used to reach overhead gas fixtures. Typically 30 inches long and equipped with a key to activate the gas and a taper to ignite the gas, it was an essential tool in a building illuminated by gas.

GIRANDOLE. A branched candleholder commonly attached to looking glasses or other reflective surfaces in the 18th and early 19th centuries. In the 1840s through the 1860s in America, the term was applied to inexpensive, freestanding, prism-hung candleholders often sold in sets and used on middle-class American mantels. The main parts were cast in metal to represent historical or popular figures from literature and attached to small marble pedestals. Many surviving examples can be found, and some bear the marks of Cornelius and Baker and Archer and Warner, major Philadelphia manufacturers.

HOLOPHANE SHADE. A clear glass shade with grooves to refract and diffuse electric light that was popular in the first decades of the 20th century.

HORN LANTERN (LANTHORN). A lantern with translucent panes made by flattening and scraping cattle horn.

KEROSENE. Hydrocarbon lamp fuel distilled from bitumen by Abraham Gesner of Nova Scotia and patented in 1854. From the Greek *keroselaion*, meaning wax-oil. It did not become widely used until after the opening of the first oil field in Pennsylvania in 1859, thereafter replacing whale oil, lard oil and burning fluid as the most common lighting fuel where gas and electricity were not available.

LANTERN. Any enclosure, e.g., of glass, horn or pierced metal, designed to prevent a small oil lamp or candle from being extinguished while permitting light to escape, either portable or fixed to a ceiling or wall.

LARD OIL. Lamp fuel rendered from the fat of swine. It became a popular American replacement for more expensive whale oil, especially in the 1840s after development of the solar lamp.

LUMINAIRE. A term used by modern manufacturers for the lamp attached to a streetlight post.

LUSTRE. A chandelier, lamp or candleholder with hanging glass prisms or pendants.

MANTEL LAMP. A popular and decorative lamp for parlor mantels of the 1830s based on the original design of Ami Argand and using his burner. Mantel lamps were frequently found in sets of three: two with single burners flanking one with two burners. Originally designed to burn whale oil, they often were converted to use kerosene and have survived in relatively large numbers.

MANTLE. A small baglike attachment on a Welsbach burner that is made of cotton gauze impregnated with oxides of rare earth. When lighted, the cotton burns away, leaving a fragile skeleton of rare earth that can be heated to incandescence.

MODERATOR LAMP. A mechanical lamp invented in France in the 1830s that used a spring-driven piston to force oil to the burner, thus moderating the flow. Always expensive, moderator lamps were uncommon in America.

PAN LIGHT. An inexpensive electric socket holder commonly used in bedrooms and middle-class parlors of the 1920s.

PENDANT. A simple electric fixture from the early 20th century, usually consisting of a drop cord and socket.

PIERCED-TIN LANTERN. A lantern with a cylindrical sheet-iron body pierced by small holes with a conical top and looped handle. This type was popular well into the 19th century.

RAPE SEED OIL. *See* colza oil.

REPOUSSÉ. Ornamental relief created by hammering from the inner side of metals.

REPRODUCTION. A fixture produced from a document.

SCONCE. A wall bracket to hold one or more candles or oil lamps, often decorative and occasionally equipped with a reflective back; also sometimes affixed to a piece of furniture such as a looking glass. Occasionally known as an arm, branch or girandole.

SINUMBRA LAMP. An early 19th-century lamp patented in France in 1820 that used an Argand burner and an annular fuel reservoir similar to the astral lamp. However, the reservoir in cross section was wedge shaped, so little shadow was cast. Because they were ostensibly shadowless, sinumbra (from the Latin, *sine umbra*, and French, *sinombre*), lamps were popular in the 1820s and 1830s when affixed to tall bases for use on parlor center tables and as ceiling fixtures hung from chains.

SMOKE BELL. Commonly a glass dish or bell suspended over the open flame of a candle or burner to protect the ceiling from carbon deposits. These were found particularly on hall lanterns and gaseliers.

SNUFFER. A scissorlike implement used to remove the charred part (snuff) of candlewicks to prevent guttering; not to be confused with a douter or extinguisher.

SOLAR LAMP. The ubiquitous American lamp of the Argand-burner type in the 1840s and 1850s. Designed to burn inexpensive lard oil, solar ("bright as the sun") lamps encased the burner in a reservoir shaped roughly like a pear balanced on its small end. Above the burner was a cap that restricted the flame to make it burn more efficiently and to transmit heat to the reservoir. The heat of the flame softened the lard oil so it would flow up the wick. These lamps were used for center-table task lighting, chandeliers, wall brackets and hanging fixtures and often were embellished with hanging prisms and required both a glass chimney and shade. The many surviving antiques may have been converted to burn kerosene.

SPERMACETI. A waxy residue rendered from the oil of the sperm whale that makes superior candles.

SPERM OIL. The most expensive lamp oil, procured from the sperm whale.

WELSBACH BURNER. A major advance in gas lighting technology that produced a hot flame and used a mantle that became incandescent, giving off a bright light. Invented about 1885, this burner was used in America from about 1890 until it was replaced by electricity, although it continues to be used in portable camp lanterns. *See also* mantle.

An (*) indicates the most important publication for a basic reading list on the subject.

*Bacot, H. Parrott. *Nineteenth-Century Lighting: Candle Powered Devices, 1783–1883*. Exton, Pa.: Schiffer Publishing, 1987.

Baroni, Daniele. *The Electric Light: A Century of Design*. New York: Van Nostrand Reinhold, 1983.

Briggs, Rose. "Pilgrim Lighting from Old Colony Inventories, 1633–1649," *The Rushlight*, August 1956, p. 2.

Brown, C. N. *J. W. Swan and the Invention of the Incandescent Electric Lamp*. London: Science Museum, 1978.

Brown, Sanborn C. "Rumford Lamps," *Proceedings of the American Philosophical Society*, February 1952, pp. 37–44.

*Butler, Joseph T. *Candleholders in America, 1650–1900*. New York: Crown Publishers, 1967.

*Caspall, John. *Making Fire and Light in the Home Pre-1820*. Woodbridge, England: Antique Collectors' Club, 1987.

Chandler, Dean. *Outline of History of Lighting by Gas*. London: South Metropolitan Gas Company, 1936.

Cook, Melissa L., and Maximilian L. Ferro, "Electric Lighting and Wiring in Historic American Buildings," *Technology and Conservation*, Spring 1983, pp. 28–48.

Cooke, Lawrence S., ed. *Lighting in America: From Colonial Rushlights to Victorian Chandeliers*. 1976. Rev. ed. Pittstown, N.J.: Main Street Press, 1984.

Cuffley, Peter. *A Complete Catalogue and History of Oil and Kerosene Lamps in Australia*. Victoria, Australia: Pioneer Design Studio, 1973.

D'Allemagne, Henry-René. *Historie du luminaire*. Paris, 1891.

*Darbee, Herbert C. *A Glossary of Old Lamps*. Technical Leaflet Series, no. 10. Nashville, Tenn.: American Association for State and Local History, 1965.

Dietz, Ulysses G., ed. *Victorian Lighting: The Dietz Catalogue of 1860*. Reprint. Watkins Glen, N.Y.: American Life Foundation, 1982.

*Duncan, Alastair. *Art Nouveau and Art Deco Lighting*. New York: Simon and Schuster, 1978.

Editors of the Pyne Press. *Lamps and Other Lighting*

Devices, 1850–1906. Princeton, N.J.: Pyne Press, 1972.

*Ferro, Maximilian, and Melissa L. Cook. *Electric Wiring and Lighting in Historic American Buildings: Guidelines for Restoration and Rehabilitation Projects.* New Bedford, Mass.: AFC, 1984.

Freeman, Larry. *New Light on Old Lamps.* Watkins Glen, N.Y.: Century House, 1968.

Gould, G. Glen. *Period Lighting Fixtures.* New York: Dodd, Mead, 1928.

Grove, John Robert. *Antique Brass Candlesticks, 1450–1750.* Queen Anne, Md., 1967.

Hayward, Arthur H. *Colonial Lighting.* 1927. 3rd ed. New York: Dover Publications, 1962. This edition contains a supplement on colonial chandeliers by James R. Marsh.

Hebard, Helen B. *Early Lighting in New England, 1620–1861.* Rutland, Vt.: Charles Tuttle, 1964.

Henriot, Gabriel. *Encyclopedia of Lighting Instruments.* 1933–34. Reprint. New York: Dover Publications, 1973.

Hough, Walter. *Collection of Heating and Lighting Utensils in the United States National Museum.* United States National Museum Bulletin 141. 1928. Reprint. Wethersfield, Conn.: Rushlight Club, 1981.

Ilin, M. *Turning Night into Day: The Story of Lighting.* Philadelphia: J. B. Lippincott, 1936.

James M'Ewan and Company. *Illustrated Catalogue of Furnishing and General Ironmongery.* Reprint. Melbourne, Australia.

Laing, Alastair. *Lighting.* London. Victoria and Albert Museum, 1982.

Little, Nina Fletcher. "References to Lighting in Colonial Records," *The Rushlight*, March 1941, pp. 5–10.

Loudon, John C. *An Encyclopedia of Cottage, Farm, and Villa Architecture and Furniture.* London, 1833.

Martens, Rachel. *The How-to Book of Repairing, Rewiring and Restoring Lamps and Lighting Fixtures.* Garden City, N.Y.: Doubleday, 1979.

Meadows, Cecil A. *Discovering Oil Lamps.* Aylesbury, England: Shire Publications, 1972.

Mitchell Vance and Company. *Picture Book of Authentic

Mid-Victorian Gas Lighting Fixtures. c. 1876. Reprint. Introduction to the new edition by Denys Peter Myers. New York: Dover Publications, 1984.

Moss, Roger W. *Identification of 19th-Century Domestic Lighting*. Slide-tape program. Nashville, Tenn.: American Association for State and Local History, 1982.

*Myers, Denys Peter. *Gaslighting in America: A Guide for Historic Preservation*. Washington, D.C.: National Park Service, U.S. Department of the Interior, 1978. Reprint. New York: Dover Publications, 1989.

Nutting, Wallace. *Furniture of the Pilgrim Century*, pp. 554–71. Boston, 1921.

————. *Furniture Treasury*, vol. 2, plates 4103–357. New York, 1928.

*O'Dea, W. T. *The Social History of Lighting*. London: Routledge and Kegan Paul, 1958.

————. *Lighting 1: Early Oil Lamps, Candles*. London: Science Museum, 1966.

. *Lighting 2: Gas, Mineral Oil, Electricity*. London: Science Museum, 1967.

Perry, David H. *Out of Darkness*. Rochester, N.Y.: Rochester Museum and Science Center, 1969.

Phillips, Derek. *Planning Your Lighting*. London: Design Center, 1976.

Poese, Bill. *Lighting Through the Years*. Des Moines: Wallace-Homestead Book Company, 1976.

Rapp, Betty. "Researching Probate Inventories for Lighting," *The Rushlight*, September 1987, pp. 10–11.

Rushlight Club. *Early Lighting*. Boston: Author, 1972.

Robins, Frederick W. *The Story of the Lamp (and the Candle)*. London and New York: Oxford University Press, 1939.

*Russell, Loris S. *A Heritage of Light*. Toronto: University of Toronto Press, 1968.

————. "Early Nineteenth-Century Lighting." In *Building Early America*. Charles E. Peterson, ed. Radnor, Pa.: Chilton Book Company, 1976.

*Schrøder, Michael. *The Argand Burner: Its Origin and Development in France and England, 1780–1803*. Copenhagen: Odense University Press, 1969.

Smith, Elmer L. *Tinware: Yesterday and Today*. Lebanon, Pa.: Applied Arts, 1974.

*Thuro, Catherine M. V. *Oil Lamps*. Des Moines: Homestead Book Company, 1976.

*———. *Oil Lamps II*. Toronto: Thorncliffe House, 1983.

Thwing, Leroy L. *Flickering Flames*. Rutland, Vt.: Charles E. Tuttle, 1958.

———. *Old Lamps of Central Europe and Other Lighting Devices*. Rutland, Vt.: Charles E. Tuttle, 1963.

———, and Julius Daniels. *A Dictionary of Old Lamps and Other Lighting Devices*. Cambridge, Mass., 1952.

Van Rensselaer, Stephen. "American Tin Candle Sconces," *Antiques*, August 1936, pp. 58–59.

Wadsworth Atheneum. *Let There Be Light*. Hartford, Conn.: Author, 1964.

Watkins, C. Malcolm. *Artificial Lighting in America, 1830–1860*. Smithsonian Report for 1951. Washington, D.C.: Smithsonian Institution, 1952.

Webster, Thomas, and Mrs. Parkes. *An Encyclopedia of Domestic Economy*. London, 1844.

The leading journal in the field of lighting history is *The Rushlight*, published by the Rushlight Club, Old Academy Library, 150 Main Street, Wethersfield, Conn. 06109. Founded in 1932, the Rushlight Club is a nonprofit organization whose purpose is to stimulate interest in the study of early lighting devices and lighting fuels and the origin and development of each, by means of articles, lectures, conferences and exhibits from private collections. The club maintains a reference library open to the public and regularly publishes books and reprints on lighting history.

THE ATHENAEUM OF PHILADELPHIA. East Washington Square, Philadelphia, Pa. 19106

COLONIAL WILLIAMSBURG FOUNDATION. P.O. Box C, Williamsburg, Va. 23185

COOPER-HEWITT MUSEUM. Smithsonian Institution, 2 East 91st Street, New York, N.Y. 10028

HAGLEY MUSEUM AND LIBRARY. P.O. Box 3630, Wilmington, Del. 19807

HENRY FORD MUSEUM AND GREENFIELD VILLAGE. 20900 Oakwood Boulevard, Dearborn, Mich. 48121

HISTORIC DEERFIELD. Deerfield, Mass. 01342

METROPOLITAN MUSEUM OF ART. 82nd Street and Fifth Avenue, New York, N.Y. 10028

NATIONAL MUSEUM OF AMERICAN HISTORY. Smithsonian Institution, 14th Street and Constitution Avenue, N.W., Washington, D.C. 20560

NEW YORK STATE HISTORICAL ASSOCIATION. P.O. Box 800, Cooperstown, N.Y. 13326

OLD STURBRIDGE VILLAGE. Route 20, Sturbridge, Mass. 01566

ROYAL ONTARIO MUSEUM-LIBRARY. 100 Queen's Park, Toronto, Ontario M5S 2C6, Canada

RUSHLIGHT CLUB. Old Academy Library, 150 Main Street, Wethersfield, Conn. 06109

SHELBURNE MUSEUM. Shelburne, Vt. 05482

SLEEPY HOLLOW RESTORATIONS (HISTORIC HUDSON VALLEY). 150 White Plains Road, Tarrytown, N.Y. 10591

SOCIETY FOR THE PRESERVATION OF NEW ENGLAND ANTIQUITIES. 141 Cambridge Street, Boston, Mass. 02114

STRONG MUSEUM. One Manhattan Square, Rochester, N.Y. 14607

VICTORIA AND ALBERT MUSEUM. Exhibition and Cromwell Roads, London SW 1, England

WADSWORTH ATHENEUM. 600 Main Street, Hartford, Conn. 06103

WINTERTHUR MUSEUM. Route 52, Kennett Pike, Winterthur, Del. 19735

ACKNOWLEDG-
MENTS

The author gratefully acknowledges the generous assistance of all the manufacturers, suppliers and dealers mentioned in this book who provided information and illustrations. Thanks are also due to curators and librarians of the institutions mentioned in the captions for their help with illustrations for the historical essays, especially bibliographer Keith A. Kamm and archivist Bruce Laverty at The Athenaeum of Philadelphia. All photographs of material from The Athenaeum collection are by Lewis Meehan.

There is no adequate way of thanking Dr. Samuel J. Dornsife, who first introduced the author to the joys and complexity of historic lighting. This book is dedicated to him.

The Preservation Press is grateful for the support and assistance of Jeffrey Pocock and Progress Lighting in the production of this book.

Lighting for Historic Buildings was developed and edited by Diane Maddex, director, The Preservation Press, with editorial assistance from Rachel Cox and production assistance from Janet Walker, managing editor, The Preservation Press.

The book was designed by Meadows & Wiser, Washington, D.C., under the direction of Marc Meadows, Robert Wiser and Mary Brown. It was composed in Cloister Old Style by BG Composition, Inc., Baltimore, and printed by Science Press, Ephrata, Pa.

ROGER W. MOSS is executive director of The Athenaeum of Philadelphia and a member of the faculty, Historic Preservation Program, Graduate School of Fine Arts, University of Pennsylvania. His other books include *Century of Color* (1981), *The Biographical Dictionary of Philadelphia Architects, 1700–1930* (1985) and, with Gail Caskey Winkler, *Victorian Interior Decoration* (1986) and *Victorian Exterior Decoration* (1987). Moss also prepared the slide-tape program *Identification of 19th-Century Domestic Lighting* (1982).

AUTHOR

Other books in this series include:

HISTORIC INTERIORS SERIES

FABRICS FOR HISTORIC BUILDINGS. Jane C. Nylander. A primer with a catalog listing 550 fabric reproductions for curtains, upholstery, bed hangings, table covers and other uses. 160 pages, 95 illus., gloss., biblio., append. $14.95 paperbound.

FLOOR COVERINGS FOR HISTORIC BUILDINGS. Helene Von Rosenstiel and Gail Caskey Winkler. A handbook on the history of American floors and carpets with a catalog of 475 reproductions suitable for historic buildings and period interiors. 284 pages, 175 illus., gloss., biblio., append. $14.95 paperbound.

WALLPAPERS FOR HISTORIC BUILDINGS. Richard C. Nylander. A guide to 350 wallpaper reproductions with advice on choosing the correct pattern. 128 pages, 110 illus., gloss., biblio., append. $14.95 paperbound.